The Complete Mueller Pressure Cooker Cookbook

Quick & Easy Müeller Pressure Cooker Recipes For Everyone

Emma Saunders

Copyright © 2017 by Emma Saunders

All rights reserved worldwide.

ISBN: 978-1730754296

No part of this book may be reproduced or transmited in any form or by any means, electronic or mechanical, including photocopying, recording or by any information storage and retrieval system, without written permission from the publisher, except for the inclusion of brief quotations in a review.

Warning-Disclaimer

The purpose of this book is to educate and entertain. The author or publisher does not guarantee that anyone following the techniques, suggestions, tips, ideas, or strategies will become successful. The author and publisher shall have neither liability or responsibility to anyone with respect to any loss or damage caused, or alleged to be caused, directly or indirectly by the information contained in this book.

Contents

INTRODUCTION 7

WHAT IS A MUELLER PRESSURE COOKER? 8

BREAKFAST & BRUNCH RECIPES 10

Rich Grits with Gruyere Cheese and Bacon 10
Poached Eggs on Heirloom Tomatoes 11
Awesome Giant Pancakes 12
Egg, Sausage & Cheese Bundt Cake 13
Salmon Veggie Cakes with Potato Salad 14

STEW, SOUPS & CHILI RECIPES 15

Chicken & Bacon Noodle Soup 15
Creamy Butternut and Cauliflower Soup 16
Crème de la Broc 17
Healthy Beef Taco Soup 18
Mustardy Beef Brisket Stew with Vegetables 19
White Wine Seafood Stew with Andouille Sausage 20
Colorful Veggie Stew 21
Creamy Chicken Stew with Mushrooms & Spinach 22
Quick and Easy Cannellini Bean Chicken Chili 23
Spicy Beef Chili with Worcestershire Sauce 24
Meatless Chipotle Chile with Walnuts 25
Pork and Sweet Potato Chili 26

CHICKEN RECIPES 28

Italian-Style Lemon Chicken 28
Creamy Chicken Breasts with Basil Pesto 29
Chicken and Wild Rice Taco Bowls 30
Spicy-Sweet Shredded Chicken 31
Coq Au Vin 32

Coconut Chicken Curry 34

Easy Chicken Thighs in Tomato Sauce 35

Buffalo Chicken Soup 36

Classic Tuscan Chicken 37

Gorgeous Chicken Fajitas with Guacamole 38

Mediterranean Meatballs Primavera..39

Greek-Style Stuffed Chicken 40

Sticky Barbecue Drumettes 41

Balsamic Thyme Chicken Thighs 42

Holiday Stuffed Full Chicken 43

PORK 44

Exciting Pork Chops with Mushroom Gravy 44

Honey-Mustard Pork Tenderloin 45

Pork Roast with Herb Gravy 46

Ginger and Garlic Pork Tenderloin with Soy Sauce..47

Quick Pork Roast Sandwich with Slaw...48

Terrific Homemade BBQ Ribs..49

Heavenly Bangers with Mashed Potatoes & Onion Gravy 50

Greek Tender Pork Roast 51

Braised Pork Neck Bones 52

Gingery Pork with Coconut Sauce...53

Mustardy Pork Loin with Vegetable Sauce 54

Pork Roast with Spicy Peanut Sauce 55

Spiced Pork Carnitas in Lettuce Cups 56

Savory Ham with Collard Greens 57

Creamy Ranch Pork Chops..58

BEEF RECIPES 59

Juicy Beef & Broccoli..59

Russian Beefy Unstuffed Cabbage Stew 60

Hoagie Beef Burgers with Provolone Cheese 61
Tricolor Pepper Rolled Beef with Onion Gravy 62
Asian-Style Red Beef Curry 63
Delicious Pepper Beef Mix 64
Bacon Wrapped Beef with Green Beans 65
Traditionally-Made Beef Bourguignonne 66
Minute Steak and Cheesy Stuffed Mushrooms 67
Savory Classic Pot Roast 68
Savory Beer Beef Stew 69
Beef Meatballs in Spaghetti Sauce 70
Original Beef Burger with Cheddar 71
Coconut Beef Roast 72
Italian Pepperoncini Beef 73

FISH RECIPES 74

Spicy and Sweet Mahi Mahi 74
Pernod-Flavored Mackerel & Vegetables en Papillote 75
One-Pot Monk Fish with Power Greens 76
Lime-Saucy Salmon 77
Fennel Alaskan Cod with Pinto Beans 78

SEAFOOD RECIPES 79

Chili-Garlic Black Mussels 79
Stylish Scottish Seafood Curry 80
Famous Carolina Crab Soup 82
Creamy Garlicky Oyster Stew 83
Seared Scallops with Butter-Caper Sauce 84

VEGETABLES & VEGETARIAN RECIPES 85

Creamy Broccoli Mash 85
Sweet Spaghetti Squash with Spinach-Walnut Pesto 86
Greek-Style Eggplant Lasagna 87

- Flavorful Leafy Green Sauté 88
- Winter Celeriac Pumpkin Soup.. 89
- Jeweled Quinoa-Stuffed Red Peppers 90
- Steamed Asparagus with Pomegranate and Pine Nuts... 91
- Spicy Zoodle and Bok Choy Soup 92
- Fall Portobello Mushroom Pilaf... 93
- Korean-Style Tofu Noddle Soup 94
- Restaurant-Style Parmesan Stuffed Mushrooms 95
- Winter Minestrone Soup.. 96
- Creamy and Greeny Soup 97

SNACKS & APPETIZERS RECIPES 98

- Finger-Licking Barbecue Chicken Wings...98
- Traditional Pao de Queijo 99
- Buffalo Chicken Balls with Roquefort Sauce 100
- Party Egg Brulee 101
- Easy Tomato-Basil Dip 102
- Bacon Wrapped Cheese Bombs 102
- Honey-Mustard Sausage Weenies 103
- Prosciutto Wrapped Asparagus 104
- Crunchy Bacon Cheeseburger Dip 104
- Cheesy Chicken Dip 105

DESSERTS RECIPES 106

- Holiday Chocolate Cheesecake 106
- Easy Crème Brulee 108
- Hot Lava Cake..109
- Lemon-Ricotta Cheesecake with Strawberry 110
- Beautiful Vanilla Pudding with Berries 111

Introduction

If you are looking for, whipping up delicious, nutritious and tasty meals with a single touch of a button, then you need a multi-cooker that can cook as a slow cooker as well as a pressure cooker. The Mueller Pressure cooker does just that - it serves not only as a slow cooker but also as a fast and efficient electric pressure cooker. Spend less time in your kitchen and enjoy the company of your loved ones while The Mueller pressure cooker takes care of your dinner.

The Mueller pressure cooker combines the functions of a pressure cooker and a slow cooker making it the perfect multi-cooker for your kitchen. It and can also steam, sauté or brown, all in a single kitchen appliance. A little too much information for you? Don't worry, as this cookbook will guide you through the process of taking advantage of your Mueller Pressure Cooker.

It encompasses a wide variety of recipes, very easy to follow and most importantly, very easy to cook in your Mueller Pressure cooker multi-cooker.

Why this cookbook?

This cookbook is meant to be a guide to you as you explore the novelty of the Mueller Pressure Cooker. My goal is that you will be able to make some sumptuous healthy meals without the pain of spending many hours in the kitchen.

You will find that the ingredients used are very easy to find and the processes are straightforward to follow which should make you have a fantastic time cooking.

Most of the recipes cook in less than an hour which is the main reason why the Mueller Pressure Cooker was invented - which is to cook a few minutes faster even than an Instant Pot.

I hope you have an exciting time blending ingredients to give your dishes that will boost your health needs.

What is a Mueller Pressure Cooker?

So, we all want things done in the fastest possible time due to heavy schedules everywhere. Totally understood and this is what this device is for – to cook foods that will require hours in just a few minutes.

It is an all-in-one cooking device that is very ready when you are while offering various cooking functions for you to cook just about anything in one pot. To top it all, these functions are pre-setted to aid a beginner cook in determining the right timings for cooking varying dishes.

Once you become a pro at it, you can alter the time settings to grant you your exact needs.

What are the Benefits of the Mueller Pressure Cooker?

Apart from the fact that the Mueller pressure cooker is a fast cooking device, it is beneficial in so many other ways.

Reduced cholesterol for cooking – You necessarily do not need a lot of oil when cooking, as the food mainly cooks with pressure or steam. If you need to use oil, then olive oil, coconut oil, and their kinds are the best for it as they are not cholesterol loaded.

One – Step Prep – Basically, all you will be doing is throwing the ingredients into the pot, closing it, and cooking it under pressure. Some recipes require an alteration in the steps but they somewhat sum up to be a one-step process in the end. It is that straightforward.

Easy to Use – The pot comes with various cooking settings that only require you to select a function, set the time at which you want the food to cook for, and then on you go with the cook. This simplifies the cooking process and makes it less stressful to use.

Energy Saving – Your bills aren't going to shoot up just because you are using a highly effective appliance. Instead, it saves on power making it more ideal to use than an electric cooker.

Cooks Everything – Yes, exactly! The Mueller pressure cooker cooks just every ingredient with various settings designed to prepare different food types to perfection. No need to worry about how high or low the heat should be for the best cook; it is handled by this one appliance. Isn't that cool?

How to Use a Mueller Pressure Cooker

- Firstly, open the Mueller pressure cooker and add all the ingredients. Place the lid back on top making sure that the cover aligns with the lock.

- Then, turn on the pot and select the cooking function you wish to cook at.

- Lock and seal the lid, and select your desired cooking time using the + and – buttons.

- Next, press START to start the cooking process.

- After the timer has read to the end, the cooker will be automatically switched to the KEEP WARM setting and press it to CANCEL.

- Proceed to dish your food from here or close the lid and keep the food warm until you're ready.

PLEASE NOTE: The cooking times are approximate values, achieved under controlled cooking. The cooking times may vary depending on the quantity and texture of the ingredients, as well as, the exact type of pressure cooker.

BREAKFAST & BRUNCH RECIPES

Rich Grits with Gruyere Cheese and Bacon

A milky cheesy grits dish has always been my favorite heavy breakfast option. They are tasty and satisfying; I skip brunch and snacks when I take them. Making them with my new Mueller pressure cooker makes life easier and faster, and I bet it will work for you too.

Preparation Time: 10 minutes | Cooking Time: 10 minutes | Servings: 4

Ingredients:

3 slices smoked Bacon, diced
1 ½ cups grated Gruyères Cheese
1 cup ground Grits
2 tsp Butter
Salt and Black Pepper
½ cup Water
½ cup Milk

Directions:

- Select Sauté mode and cook bacon until crispy, about 5 minutes.
- Set aside. Add the grits, butter, milk, water, salt, and pepper to the pot and stir using a spoon. Close the lid and secure the pressure valve.
- Select the Manual mode on High pressure for 10 minutes.
- Once the timer has ended, do a quick pressure release again.
- Immediately add the cheddar cheese and give the pudding a good stir using the same spoon.
- Dish the cheesy grits into serving bowls and spoon over the crisped bacon.
- Serve right away with toasted bread.

Nutrition facts per serving:

Calories 280; Fat 20.6g; Sodium 325mg; Carbs 8g; Protein 13.8g

Poached Eggs on Heirloom Tomatoes

You almost can't tear poached eggs away from brunch because they are always the perfect items to have. Now, you do not need to worry about disappointments from the stove top, just set the Mueller pressure cooker right and your brunch table will be beaming with goodness.

Preparation Time: 7 minutes | Cooking Time: 3 minutes | Servings: 4

Ingredients:

4 large Eggs
2 cups Water
2 large Heirloom Tomatoes, halved crosswise
Salt and Black Pepper to taste
1 tsp chopped Fresh Herbs, of your choice
2 tbsp grated Parmesan Cheese

Special Tools:
Cooking Spray
4 small Ramekins
Trivet

Directions:

- Pour the water in and fit a trivet at the center of the pot.
- Grease the ramekins with the cooking spray and crack each egg into them.
- Place the ramekins on the trivet. Close the lid.
- Turn on the Mueller, select Steam mode for 3 minutes on High.
- Once the timer goes off, press Cancel, do a quick pressure release.
- Use a napkin to remove the ramekins onto a flat surface.
- In serving plates, share the halved heirloom tomatoes and toss the eggs in the ramekin over on each tomato half.
- Sprinkle with salt and pepper, parmesan, and garnish with chopped herbs.

Nutrition facts per serving:

Calories 123; Fat 6.9g; Sodium 147mg; Carbs 7.6g; Protein 6.3g

Awesome Giant Pancakes

You know how pancakes are often flat and boring sometimes, how about a bit of tweak up? This pancake is compacted with goodness and melts in your mouth at every bite. Drizzle some monk fruit syrup on it and enjoy this world of nourishment.

Preparation Time: 15 minutes | Cooking Time: 15 minutes | Servings: 6

Ingredients:

3 cups All-purpose Flour
¾ cup Sugar
5 Eggs
⅓ cup Olive Oil

⅓ cup Sparkling Water
⅓ tsp Salt
1 ½ tsp Baking Soda

To Serve:
2 tbsp Maple Syrup

A dollop of Whipped Cream

Special Tool:
Food Processor and Toothpick

Directions:

- Start by pouring the flour, sugar, eggs, olive oil, sparkling water, salt, and baking soda into the food processor and blend them until smooth.
- Pour the resulting batter into the Mueller pressure cooker and let it sit in there for 15 minutes.
- Close the lid and secure the pressure valve.
- Turn on the Mueller Cooker, select the Manual mode on Low pressure for 15 minutes.
- Once the timer goes off, press Cancel, release the pressure valve to let out any steam and open the lid.
- Stick in a toothpick, and once it comes out clean, the pancake is done.
- Gently run a spatula around the pancake to let loose any sticking.
- Then, slide the pancakes into a serving plate.
- Top with the whipped cream and drizzle the maple syrup over it to serve.

Nutrition facts per serving:

Calories 432; Fat 15.6g; Sodium 133mg; Carbs 59.1g; Protein 11.3g

Egg, Sausage & Cheese Bundt Cake

I can't get enough excitement out of this "sweet" mix. Rather than having regular boiled eggs, or scrambled eggs, make this casserole loaded with protein, sweet peppers, and some early morning spice.

Preparation Time: 15 minutes | Cooking Time: 8 minutes | Servings: 6

Ingredients:

8 Eggs, cracked into a bowl
8 oz Breakfast Sausage, chopped
3 Bacon Slices, chopped
1 large Green Bell Pepper, chopped
1 large Red Bell Pepper, chopped
1 cup chopped Green Onion
1 cup grated Cheddar Cheese
1 tsp Red Chili Flakes
Salt and Black Pepper to taste
½ cup Milk
4 slices Bread, cut into ½-inch cubes
2 cups Water

Special Tools:
Bundt Pan (to fit into the Mueller pressure cooker), Cooking Spray and Trivet

Directions:

- Add the eggs, sausage, bacon slices, green bell pepper, red bell pepper, green onion, red chili flakes, cheddar cheese, salt, pepper, and milk to a bowl and use a whisk to beat them together.
- Grease the bundt pan with cooking spray and pour the egg mixture into it. After, drop the bread slices in the egg mixture all around while using a spoon to push them into the mixture.
- Open the Mueller Cooker, pour in water, and fit the trivet at the center of the pot. Place bundt pan on the trivet and seal the lid.
- Select Steam mode on High for 8 minutes. Once the timer goes off, press Keep Warm/Cancel to cancel, and do a quick pressure release.
- Use a napkin to gently remove the bundt pan onto a flat surface.
- Run a knife around the egg in the bundt pan, place a serving plate on the bundt pan, and then, turn the egg bundt over.
- Use a knife to cut the egg into slices. Serve with sauce of your choice.

Nutrition facts per serving:

Calories 381; Fat 26.9g; Sodium 450mg; Carbs 14.2g; Protein 24g

Salmon Veggie Cakes with Potato Salad

How about you leave salmon off the dinner list tomorrow and have it late in the morning? Sounds like a great idea, right? These cakes are made with veggies and some aromatic spices to set your mood up for the rest of the day's work.

Preparation Time: 10 minutes | Cooking Time: 30 minutes | Servings: 4

Ingredients:

2 (5 oz) packs Steamed Salmon Flakes
1 Red Onion, chopped
Salt and Black Pepper to taste
1 tsp Garlic Powder
2 tbsp Olive Oil
1 Red Bell Pepper, seeded and chopped
4 tbsp Butter, divided
3 Eggs, cracked into a bowl
1 cup Breadcrumbs
4 tbsp Mayonnaise
2 tsp Worcestershire Sauce
¼ cup chopped Parsley

Directions:

- Turn on the Mueller pressure cooker and select Sauté mode.
- Heat the oil and add half of the butter. Once it has melted, add the onions and the chopped red bell peppers. Cook for 9 minutes while stirring occasionally.
- After 9 minutes, press Cancel. In a mixing bowl, add the salmon flakes, sautéed red bell pepper, sautéed onion, breadcrumbs, eggs, mayonnaise, Worcestershire sauce, garlic powder, salt, pepper, and parsley.
- Use a spoon to mix them well while breaking the salmon into the smallest possible pieces.
- Use your hands to mold 4 patties out of the mixture and place them on a plate.
- Select Sauté mode on the Mueller pressure cooker and add the remaining butter. Once the butter has melted, add the patties to the oil and fry them until they are golden brown.
- Remove them onto a wire rack to rest for 2 minutes. Serve the cakes with a side of lettuce and potato salad with a mild drizzle of herb vinaigrette.

Nutrition facts per serving:

Calories 373; Fat 25.5g; Sodium 440mg; Carbs 11.2g; Protein 21.4g

STEW, SOUPS & CHILI RECIPES

Chicken & Bacon Noodle Soup

If you are looking for something that is in between light and filling for lunch, this chicken turnip soup has you in the right place. This recipe is a good way to combine carbs with some fats and proteins for a more tummy filling desire.

Preparation Time: 10 minutes | Cooking Time: 23 minutes | Servings: 8

Ingredients:

5 oz dry Egg Noodles
4 Chicken Breasts, skinless and boneless
1 large White Onion, chopped
8 Bacon Slices, chopped
4 cloves Garlic, minced
Salt and Black Pepper to taste

2 medium Carrots, sliced
2 cups sliced Celery
½ cup chopped Parsley
1 ½ tsp Dried Thyme
8 cups Chicken Broth

Directions:

— Turn on the Mueller Cooker, open the pot, and select Sauté mode. Pour the chopped bacon in it and fry them for 5 minutes until brown and crispy. Add the onion and garlic, and cook them with the bacon for 3 minutes.

— Afterward, remove both the bacon mixture with a slotted spoon onto a plate and set aside while you discard the grease in the pot too.

— Now, pour the bacon mixture back into the pot and add the chicken breasts, noodles, carrots, celery, chicken broth, thyme, salt, and pepper.

— Close the lid, secure the pressure valve, and select Manual mode on High pressure for 5 minutes.

— Once the timer has ended, do a quick pressure release, and open the lid. Use a wooden spoon to remove the chicken onto a plate. Shred the chicken with two forks and add it back to the soup. Stir well with the wooden spoon.

— Adjust the seasoning as desired and dish the soup into serving bowls. Sprinkle with cheddar cheese and serve with a side of bread.

Nutrition facts per serving:

Calories 419; Fat 19g; Sodium 640mg; Carbs 15.3g; Protein 35g

Creamy Butternut and Cauliflower Soup

Super packed with richness: proteins, vitamins, and healthy fats. This soup is so filling and delicious. The toppings make it exciting with a side of toasted bread.

Preparation Time: 15 minutes | Cooking Time: 17 minutes | Servings: 4

Ingredients:

2 tsp Olive Oil
1 large White Onion, chopped
4 cloves Garlic, minced
1 (2 pounds) Butternut Squash, peeled, seeded, and cubed
2 heads Cauliflower, cut in florets
3 cups Chicken Broth
3 tsp Paprika
Salt and Black Pepper to taste
1 cup Milk, full fat

Topping:
Grated Cheddar Cheese, Crumbled Bacon, Chopped Chives, Pumpkin Seeds

Directions:

- Turn on the Mueller Pressure Cooker, open it, and select Sauté mode.
- Heat olive oil, add the white onion and sauté it for about 3 minutes.
- Then, add the garlic and cook them until fragrant which for about 3 minutes.
- Next, pour in the butternut squash, cauliflower florets, broth, paprika, pepper, and salt (if needed because of the broth). Stir the ingredients with a spoon.
- Close the lid, secure the pressure valve and select Manual mode on High pressure for 10 minutes.
- Once the timer has ended, do a quick pressure release, and open the lid.
- Top the ingredients with the milk and use a stick blender to puree them.
- Adjust the seasoning, stir, and dish the soup into serving bowls.
- Add the toppings on the soup and serve warm.

Nutrition facts per serving:

Calories 183; Fat 5.1g; Sodium 485mg; Carbs 23.2g; Protein 10.2g

Crème de la Broc

I can't get enough of the creamy, tasty goodness that this broccoli soup has to offer. It is farfetched from a pureed green soup but rather the broccoli serves as meat chunks in the soup. You've just gotta-love-it!

Preparation Time: 10 minutes | Cooking Time: 15 minutes | Servings: 6

Ingredients:

3 cups Heavy Cream
3 cups Vegetable Broth
4 tbsp Butter
4 tbsp All-purpose Flour
4 cups chopped Broccoli Florets, only the bushy tops
1 medium Red Onion, chopped
3 cloves Garlic, minced
1 tsp Italian Seasoning
Salt and Black Pepper to taste
1 ½ oz Cream Cheese
1 ½ cups grated Yellow and White Cheddar Cheese + extra for topping

Directions:

- Select Sauté mode and add the butter to it once the pot is ready.
- Melt the butter and add the flour and use a spoon to stir it until it clumps up. Gradually pour in the heavy cream while stirring until white sauce forms. Fetch out the butter sauce into a bowl and set aside.
- Turn off the Sauté mode and add the onions, garlic, broth, broccoli, Italian seasoning, and cream cheese. Use a wooden spoon to stir the mixture.
- Seal the lid, and select Manual mode on High pressure for 15 minutes. Once the timer has ended, do a quick pressure release.
- Keep the pot in Warm mode and add butter sauce and cheddar cheese, salt, and pepper (as necessary). Stir with a spoon until the cheese has melted.
- Dish the soup into serving bowls, top it with extra cheese, to serve.

Nutrition facts per serving:

Calories 523; Fat 42.5g; Sodium 350mg; Carbs 12.1g; Protein 17.2g

Healthy Beef Taco Soup

Sounds great to have tacos night? You definitely can in soup and guess what? It tastes better. The ingredients used in this recipe are nutrient packed which are good to keep you in check on your weight loss program.

Preparation Time: 10 minutes | Cooking Time: 20 minutes | Servings: 8

Ingredients:

2 tbsp Olive Oil
6 Green Bell pepper, diced
2 medium Yellow Onion, chopped
3 lb Ground Beef, grass fed
Salt and Black Pepper to taste
3 tbsp Chili Powder
2 tbsp Cumin Powder
2 tsp Paprika

1 tsp Garlic Powder
1 tsp Cinnamon
1 tsp Onion Powder
6 cups chopped Tomatoes
½ cup chopped Green Chilies
3 cups Bone Broth
3 cups Milk

Topping:

Chopped Jalapenos, Sliced Avocados, Chopped Cilantro, Chopped Green Onions, Lime Juice

Directions:

- Turn on and open the Mueller Pressure Cooker, then, select Sauté mode.
- Pour in the oil, once it has heated add the yellow onion and green peppers. Sauté them until they are soft for about 5 minutes. Include the ground beef, stir the ingredients, and let the beef cook for about 8 minutes until it browns.
- Next, add the chili powder, cumin powder, black pepper, paprika, cinnamon, garlic powder, onion powder, and green chilies. Give them a good stir using a plastic or wooden spoon.
- Top with the tomatoes, milk, and bone broth. Stir also. Close the lid, secure the pressure valve, and select Soup on High for 20 minutes.
- Once the timer has ended, do a quick pressure release. Keep in Warm mode.
- Adjust the taste with salt and pepper. Dish the taco soup into serving bowls and add the toppings. Serve warm with a side of tortillas.

Nutrition facts per serving:

Calories 522; Fat 25.3g; Sodium 289mg; Carbs 21g; Protein 48.5g

Mustardy Beef Brisket Stew with Vegetables

This beef stew is a given when it comes to making awesome stews. The ingredients cook faster in this case especially the beef which cooks so soft to tear apart as you dig your spoon in. Enjoy this stew with the family at dinner; they'll love you without fail.

Preparation Time: 15 minutes | Cooking Time: 55 minutes | Servings: 4

Ingredients:

- 2 lb Brisket, cut into 2-inch pieces
- 4 cups Beef Broth
- Salt and Black Pepper to taste
- 1 tbsp Dijon Mustard
- 1 tbsp Olive Oil
- 1 lb small Potato, quartered
- ¼ lb Carrots, cut in 2-inch pieces
- 1 large Red Onion, quartered
- 3 cloves Garlic, minced
- 1 Bay Leaf
- 2 fresh Thyme sprigs
- 2 tbsp Cornstarch
- 3 tbsp chopped Cilantro to garnish

Directions:

- Pour the beef broth, cornstarch, Dijon mustard, ½ teaspoon salt, and ½ teaspoon pepper in a bowl.
- Mix them with a whisk and set aside.
- Season the beef strips with salt and pepper.
- Turn on the Mueller Pressure Cooker, open the lid and select Sauté mode.
- Add the olive oil, once heated include the beef strips and cook them to brown. Turn the beef halfway through the cook with a spoon.
- Once the beef has browned which is about 8 minutes, add the potato, carrots, onion, garlic, thyme, mustard mixture, and bay leaf. Stir once more.
- Close the lid, secure the pressure valve, and select Manual mode on High pressure for 45 minutes.
- Once the timer has ended, do a quick pressure release.
- Stir the stew and remove the bay leaf. Season the stew with pepper and salt.
- Serve the soup with a bread of your choice.

Nutrition facts per serving:

Calories 498; Fat 15.2g; Sodium 508mg; Carbs 32.6g; Protein 47.3g

White Wine Seafood Stew with Andouille Sausage

What a fun packed stew? Different in taste, unique in color, and loaded with nutrients that the body needs. The Mueller pressure cooker makes it quick so once you have everything in, get a quick shower, and when you are out, you should be ready to munch on some good stuff.

Preparation Time: 15 minutes | Cooking Time: 23 minutes | Servings: 8

Ingredients:

1 lb Halibut, skinless and cut into 1-inch pieces
1 lb medium Shrimp, peeled and deveined
2 lb Mussels, debearded and scrubbed
2 (16 oz) Clam Juice
6 cups Water
2 (8 oz) Andouille Sausage, fully cooked and sliced
1 cup White Wine
Salt and Black Pepper to taste
4 tbsp Olive Oil
4 cloves Garlic, minced
2 small Fennel Bulb, chopped
4 small Leeks, sliced
A little pinch Saffron
2 Bay Leaves
2 (28 oz) can Diced Tomatoes
4 tbsp chopped Parsley

Directions:

- Turn on the Mueller Pressure Cooker, open the lid, and select Sauté mode.
- Pour in the olive oil, once heated add the sausages, fennel, and leeks. Cook them for 5 minutes while stirring occasionally.
- Top with the garlic, saffron, and bay leaf. Stir constantly for 30 seconds, then, add the wine, stir the mixture again, and cook it for 2 minutes.
- Include the tomatoes, clam juice, and water. Stir it once.
- Now, add the mussels, fish, and shrimp. Use the spoon to cover them with the sauce but don't stir.
- Close the lid, secure the pressure valve, and select Meat mode on High pressure for 15 minutes.

- Once the timer has ended, do a quick pressure release, and open the lid.
- Remove the bay leaf and discard it. Add the parsley, adjust the seasoning with pepper and salt, and stir. Serve immediately with a side of garlic bread.

Nutrition facts per serving:

Calories 465; Fat 20.6g; Sodium 254mg; Carbs 37.4g; Protein 36.5g

Colorful Veggie Stew

Very simple to make but yet with top-notch taste. This stew is best enjoyed with braised bamboo shoots and fantastic to have as a vegetarian option and also for lunch.

Preparation Time: 10 minutes | Cooking Time: 23 minutes | Servings: 4

Ingredients:

3 tbsp Olive Oil
2 large White Onions, chopped
8 oz Pepperoni, sliced
2 Eggplants, cut in half moons
2 cups Vegetable Broth
2 cloves Garlic, minced

¾ lb Brussels Sprouts, halved
Salt and Black Pepper to taste
1 ½ lb Tomatoes, chopped
3 Zucchinis, quartered
¾ lb Green Beans

Directions:

- Turn on the Mueller Pressure Cooker, open the lid and select Sauté mode.
- Pour in 1 tablespoon of oil, once heated add the onions, garlic, and pepperoni. Stir and cook for 8 minutes.
- Add the remaining oil, eggplants, Brussel sprouts, tomatoes, zucchinis, green beans, broth, salt, and pepper. Stir using a spoon.
- Close the lid, secure the pressure valve, and select Meat mode on High pressure for 15 minutes.
- Once the timer has stopped, do a quick pressure release. Dish the stew into a serving bowl and serve with a side of braised bamboo shoots.

Nutrition facts per serving:

Calories 435; Fat 32.3g; Sodium 540mg; Carbs 34g; Protein 16.3g

Creamy Chicken Stew with Mushrooms & Spinach

The look of this dish will make your guests hungry in an instance. Figuring out what the best dinner stew should be when you have a few friends visiting? This is one perfect choice! Serve it to a side of buttery squash mash, and you'll be in awe at the taste.

Preparation Time: 25 minutes | Cooking Time: 31 minutes | Servings: 4

Ingredients:

4 Chicken Breasts, diced
1 ¼ lb White Button Mushrooms, halved
3 tbsp Olive Oil
1 large Onion, sliced
5 cloves Garlic, minced
Salt and Black Pepper to taste
1 ¼ tsp Cornstarch

½ cup Spinach, chopped
1 Bay Leaf
1 ½ cups Chicken Stock
1 tsp Dijon Mustard
1 ½ cup Sour Cream
3 tbsp Chopped Parsley

Directions:

- Turn on the Mueller Pressure Cooker, open the lid, and select Sauté mode.
- Once the pot is ready, add the olive oil to heat then include the onion and sauté it for 3 minutes.
- Add the mushrooms, chicken, garlic, bay leaf, salt, pepper, Dijon mustard, and chicken broth. Stir well.
- Close the lid, secure the pressure valve, and press the Meat mode on High pressure for 15 minutes.
- Once the timer has ended, do a natural pressure release for 5 minutes, then a quick pressure release to let the remaining steam out, and open the lid. Select Sauté mode again.
- Stir the stew, remove the bay leaf, and scoop some of the liquid into a bowl. Add the cornstarch to the liquid and mix them until completely lump free.
- Pour the liquid into the sauce, stir it, and let the sauce thicken to your desired consistency. Top it with the sour cream, stir the sauce, and hit Warm mode.
- After 4 minutes, dish the sauce into serving bowls and garnish it with the chopped parsley. Serve with steamed green peas.

Nutrition facts per serving:

Calories 456; Fat 26.3g; Sodium 450mg; Carbs 22g; Protein 42.1g

Quick and Easy Cannellini Bean Chicken Chili

Light and pretty to the eyes, this chicken chili goes well with any steamed vegetable dish. Make it for your lunch pack and the aromas from your bowl will earn you a lot of inquiries from your colleagues.

Preparation Time: 15 minutes | Cooking Time: 25 minutes | Servings: 4

Ingredients:

3 Chicken Breasts, cubed
3 cups Chicken Broth
1 tbsp Butter
1 White Onion, chopped
Salt and Black Pepper
2 (14.5 ounce) cans Cannellini beans, drained and rinsed
1 tsp Cumin Powder
1 tsp dried Oregano
½ cup heavy Whipping Cream
1 cup Sour Cream

Directions:

- Turn on the Mueller Pressure Cooker, open the lid and select Sauté mode.
- Put the butter in the pot to melt and then, add the onion and chicken. Stir and let the chicken cook for 6 minutes
- Stir in the cannellini beans, cumin powder, oregano, salt, and pepper.
- Pour in the broth, stir, close the lid, and secure the pressure valve.
- Select Chili mode on High pressure for 10 minutes.
- Once the timer has ended, let the pot sit uncovered for 10 minutes, then do a quick pressure release.
- Stir in the whipping and sour cream. Dish the sauce into serving bowls.
- Serve warm with a mix of steamed bell peppers and broccoli.

Nutrition facts per serving:

Calories 535; Fat 33g; Sodium 340mg; Carbs 15g; Protein 46.7g

Spicy Beef Chili with Worcestershire Sauce

I honestly can't find the right words to explain the taste of this beef chili. It follows a very simple procedure with ingredients that are very easy to find but yet the blend of juices exuded from the ingredients is mind-blowing.

Preparation Time: 12 minutes | Cooking Time: 28 minutes | Servings: 4

Ingredients:

2 lb Ground Beef
2 tbsp Olive Oil
1 large Red Bell Pepper, seeded and chopped
1 large Yellow Bell Pepper, seeded and chopped
1 White Onion, Chopped
2 cups Chopped Tomatoes
2 cups Beef Broth
2 Carrots, cut in little bits
2 tsp Onion Powder
2 tsp Garlic Powder
5 tsp Chili Powder
2 tbsp Worcestershire Sauce
2 tsp Paprika
½ tsp Cumin Powder
2 tbsp chopped Parsley
Salt and Black Pepper to taste

Directions:

- Turn on the Mueller Pressure Cooker, select Sauté mode, and add the olive oil and ground beef. Cook the meat until it browns while stirring occasionally for about 8 minutes. Top it with the remaining ingredients and mix well.
- Close the lid, secure the pressure valve, and select Chili mode on High pressure for 20 minutes. Once the timer has ended, do a quick pressure release, and open the lid. Stir the stew and dish it into serving bowls. Serve this simple beef chili with some crackers or with potato squash.

Nutrition facts per serving:

Calories 437; Fat 18.6g; Sodium 550mg; Carbs 16g; Protein 39.3g

Meatless Chipotle Chile with Walnuts

Nothing hurts to tweak an ordinary vegetable chili with some nutty flavor. In here, it is packed with rich tastes and aromas to go with a zoodle, turnip mash or steamed greens dish. Have fun indulging in the aromas and enjoy the good taste.

Preparation Time: 10 minutes | Cooking Time: 21 minutes | Servings: 4

Ingredients:

4 Celery Stalks, chopped
2 (15 oz) cans Diced Tomatoes
1 tbsp Olive Oil
3 Carrots, chopped
2 cloves Garlic, minced
2 tsp Smoked Paprika
2 Green Bell Pepper, diced
½ cup Water
1 tbsp Cinnamon Powder
1 tbsp Cumin Powder
1 Sweet Onion, chopped
2 cups Tomato Sauce
1.5 oz Dark Chocolate, chopped
1 small Chipotle, minced
1 ½ cups raw Walnuts, chopped + extra to garnish
Salt and Pepper, to taste
Chopped Cilantro to garnish

Directions:

- Turn on the Mueller Pressure Cooker, open the lid and select Sauté mode.
- Pour in the oil to heat and add the onion, celery, and carrots. Sauté them for 4 minutes.
- Add the garlic, cumin, cinnamon, and paprika. Stir them and let the sauce cook for 2 minutes.
- Then, include the bell peppers, tomatoes, tomato sauce, chipotle, water, and walnuts Stir.
- Close the lid, secure the pressure valve, and select Meat mode on High pressure for 15 minutes.
- Once the timer has ended, do a quick pressure release, and open the lid.
- Pour the chopped chocolate in and stir it until it melts and is well incorporated into the chili. Adjust the taste with salt and pepper.
- Dish the chili into a serving bowl, garnish it with the remaining walnuts and cilantro. Serve with some noodles.

Nutrition facts per serving:

Calories 387; Fat 25.7g; Sodium 222mg; Carbs 42g; Protein 15g

Pork and Sweet Potato Chili

Massive aromas gush out of this dish. I like the greeny effect it has which communicates YUMMY. I prefer to have this chili with chips or crusted bread because the satisfaction is pleasant, but you can have it with some steamed root veggies. Remember, moderation though!

Preparation Time: 5 minutes | Cooking Time: 65 minutes | Servings: 6

Ingredients:

1 ½ lb Pork Roast, cut into 1-inch cubes
1 lb Tomatillos, husks removed
2 tbsp Olive Oil, divided into 2
1 bulb Garlic, tail sliced off
2 Green Chilies
3 cups Chicken Broth
1 Green Bell Pepper, seeded and roughly chopped
Salt and Pepper, to taste
½ tsp Cumin Powder
1 tsp dried Oregano
1 Bay Leaf
1 bunch Cilantro, chopped and divided into 2
2 Sweet Potatoes, peeled and cut into ½-inch cubes

Directions:

- Preheat your oven to 450 F.
- Put the garlic bulb on a baking tray and drizzle a bit of 1 portion of olive oil over the garlic bulb.
- Place the green bell peppers, onion, green chilies, and tomatillos on the baking tray in a single layer.
- Tuck the tray in the oven and roast the veggies and spices for 25 minutes. After 25 minutes, remove them from the oven and let them cool.
- Peel the garlic using a knife and place it in a blender. Add the green bell pepper, tomatillos, onion, and green chilies to the blender. Pulse them for a few minutes not to be smooth but slightly chunky.
- Now, turn on the Mueller Pressure Cooker, open the lid, and select Sauté.

- Pour in the remaining olive oil and while the oil is heating, season the pork cubes with pepper and salt. After, add the pork to the oil and brown them for about 5 minutes. Add the oregano and cumin. Stir.
- Add the bay leaf, pour in the blended green sauce, potatoes, and add the chicken broth. Stir.
- Close the lid, secure the pressure valve, and select Manual mode on High pressure for 35 minutes.
- Once the timer has ended, let the pot sit closed for 10 minutes. After, do a natural pressure release for 5 minutes, and then a quick pressure release to let the remaining steam out. Open the pot.
- Remove and discard the bay leaf, add half of the cilantro, adjust with salt and pepper, and stir.
- Dish the chili into serving bowls and garnish it with the remaining chopped cilantro.
- Serve topped with a side of chips or crusted bread.

Nutrition facts per serving:

Calories 410; Fat 18g; Sodium 90mg; Carbs 16g; Protein 37g

CHICKEN RECIPES

Italian-Style Lemon Chicken

Zingy goodness! This one pot chicken dish is full of life. The lemon added has a magical way of kicking those happy moods up while keeping your body in the healthiest states possible. Serve these chicken pieces with a side of steamed spinach and kale mix and drizzle the sauce from it all over the dish. You will love it!

Preparation Time: 5 minutes | Cooking Time: 21 minutes | Servings: 4

Ingredients:

4 Chicken Thighs
1 ½ tbsp Olive Oil
½ tsp Garlic Powder
Salt and Black Pepper to taste
½ tsp Red Pepper Flakes
½ tsp Smoked Paprika
1 small Onion, chopped

2 cloves Garlic, sliced
½ cup Chicken Broth
1 tsp Italian Seasoning
1 Lemon, zested and juiced
1 ½ tbsp Heavy Cream
Lemon slices to garnish
Chopped parsley to garnish

Directions:

- Turn on the Mueller Pressure Cooker, open the lid, and select Sauté mode. Warm the olive oil and add the chicken thighs; cook to brown on each side for 3 minutes. Remove the browned chicken onto a plate.
- Put the butter in the pot to melt, then, add the garlic, onions, and lemon juice. Stir them with a spoon to deglaze the bottom of the pot and let them cook for 1 minute. Add the Italian seasoning, chicken broth, lemon zest, and the chicken. Close the lid, secure the pressure valve, select Poultry mode on High pressure for 15 minutes.
- Once the timer has ended, let the pot sit closed for 2 minutes, then do a quick pressure release. Open the lid.
- Remove the chicken onto a plate and add the heavy cream to the pot. Select Sauté mode and stir the cream into the sauce until it thickens.
- Turn off the cooker and return the chicken. Coat the chicken with sauce.
- Dish the sauce into a serving platter and serve with the steamed kale and spinach mix. Garnish with the lemons slices and parsley.

Nutrition facts per serving:

Calories 487; Fat 36g; Sodium 268mg; Carbs 8g; Protein 28g

Creamy Chicken Breasts with Basil Pesto

Can we ever get tired of tasty creamy dishes? Not me I'm sure. This cream infused chicken dish is not only tasty but very healthy for most dieting needs. I love it when the children splurge over it on noodles, but for me, I enjoy it over a mix of spiralized vegetables.

Preparation Time: 3 minutes | Cooking Time: 27 minutes | Servings: 4

Ingredients:

4 Chicken Breasts, skinless and boneless
½ cup Heavy Cream
½ cup Chicken Broth
⅓ tsp minced Garlic
Salt and Black Pepper to taste
⅓ tsp Italian Seasoning
¼ cup Roasted Red Peppers
1 tbsp Basil Pesto
1 tbsp Cornstarch

Directions:

- Open the Mueller Pressure Cooker and put the chicken at the bottom of it.
- Pour the chicken broth over it and add the Italian seasoning, garlic, salt, and pepper. Close the lid, secure the pressure valve, and select Poultry mode on High pressure for 15 minutes.
- Once the timer has ended, do a natural pressure release for 5 minutes, then a quick pressure release to let the remaining steam out, and open the pot.
- Use a spoon to remove the chicken onto a plate and select Sauté mode on the pot. Scoop out any fat or unwanted chunks from the sauce.
- In a small bowl, add the cream, cornstarch, red peppers, and pesto. Mix them with a spoon.
- Pour the creamy mixture into the pot and whisk it for 4 minutes until it is well mixed and thickened. Put the chicken back in the pot and let it simmer for 3 minutes. Turn the pot off and dish the sauce onto a serving platter.
- Serve the chicken with sauce over a bed of cooked quinoa.

Nutrition facts per serving:

Calories 372; Fat 19g; Sodium 497mg; Carbs 5g; Protein 35g

Chicken and Wild Rice Taco Bowls

So right here is a cookbook that champions tacos anytime of the year. This dish is a blend of faux carbs, proteins, and lip licking tastes. Get ready to be bugged for more!

Preparation Time: 4 minutes | Cooking Time: 19 minutes | Servings: 4

Ingredients:

4 Chicken Breasts
2 cups Chicken Broth
2 ¼ packets Taco Seasoning
1 cup Wild Rice

1 Green Bell Pepper, seeded and diced
1 Red Bell Pepper, seeded and diced
1 cup Salsa
Salt and Black Pepper to taste

To Serve:

Grated Cheese, of your choice
Chopped Cilantro

Sour Cream
Avocado Slices

Directions:

- Turn on the Mueller Pressure Cooker and open the lid.
- Pour the chicken broth into the pot, add the chicken, and pour the taco seasoning over it.
- Add the salsa and stir it lightly with a spoon.
- Close the lid, secure the pressure valve, and select Poultry on High setting for 15 minutes.
- Once the timer has ended, do a quick pressure release, and open the lid.
- Add the wild rice and peppers, and use a spoon to push them into the sauce. Close the lid, secure the pressure valve, and select Steam mode on High pressure for 15 minutes.
- Once the timer has ended, do a quick pressure release, and open the lid.
- Gently stir the mixture, adjust the taste with salt and pepper and spoon the chicken dish into serving bowls.
- Top it with some sour cream, avocado slices, sprinkle with chopped cilantro and some cheese. Serve.

Nutrition facts per serving:

Calories 523; Fat 22g; Sodium 540mg; Carbs 41g; Protein 44g

Spicy-Sweet Shredded Chicken

Ok, so having a Mueller pressure cooker and not making some sweet, spicy chicken already will be under-utilizing your pot. This dish is mild on flavor but has that spicy kick to set you active the rest of the day hence the best time to have this sauce is at lunch.

Preparation Time: 7 minutes | Cooking Time: 28 minutes | Servings: 4

Ingredients:

4 Chicken Breasts, skinless
¼ cup Sriracha Sauce
2 tbsp Butter
1 tsp grated Ginger
2 cloves Garlic, minced
½ tsp Cayenne Pepper

½ tsp Red Chili Flakes
½ cup Honey
½ cup Chicken Broth
Salt and Black Pepper to taste
Chopped Scallion to garnish

Directions:

- In a bowl, pour the chicken broth. Add the honey, ginger, sriracha sauce, red pepper flakes, cayenne pepper, and garlic. Use a spoon to mix them well and set aside.
- Put the chicken on a plate and season them with salt and pepper. Set aside too. Turn on the Mueller Pressure cooker and select Sauté mode.
- Put in the butter to melt and add the chicken in 2 batches and cook them to brown on both sides for about 3 minutes.
- Add all the chicken back to the pot and pour the pepper sauce over it.
- Close the lid, secure the pressure valve, and select Poultry mode on High pressure for 20 minutes.
- Once the timer has ended, do a natural pressure release for 5 minutes, then a quick pressure release to let the remaining steam out, and open the lid.
- Remove the chicken onto a cutting board and shred them using two forks.
- Put the chicken in a serving bowl, pour the sauce over it, and garnish it with the scallions.
- Serve with a side of sauteéd mushrooms.

Nutrition facts per serving:

Calories 462; Fat 16g; Sodium 540mg; Carbs 38g; Protein 37g

Coq Au Vin

An exceptional French delicacy which cooks perfectly in the Mueller Pressure Cooker. It is a good option when you have visitors coming; however, you'll have to plan some hours ahead to get the tastes and flavors right. Your guest will love your home because of this dish.

Preparation Time: 8 hours 10 minutes | Cooking Time: 50 minutes | Servings: 4

Ingredients:

3 Chicken Legs, cut into drumsticks and thighs
2 Bacon Slices, chopped in ¾-inch pieces
1 ½ cups Dry White Wine
Salt and Black Pepper to taste
½ bunch Thyme, divided
8 oz Shiitake Mushrooms, stems removed and cut into 4 pieces
3 Shallots, peeled
3 tbsp Butter, divided
3 skinny Carrots, cut into 4 crosswise pieces each
2 cloves Garlic, crushed
1 tbsp All-purpose flour
3 tbsp chopped Parsley for garnishing

Special Tool:
Zipper Plastic Bag

Directions:

- Put the chicken on a clean flat surface and season them on both sides with salt and pepper.
- In a plastic zipper bag, pour the wine. Add half of the thyme and chicken.
- Zip the bag and shake it to coat the chicken well with the wine.
- Place it in the refrigerator for 6 to 8 hours.
- After 8 hours, turn on the Mueller Pressure cooker and add the bacon to it.
- Fry it to brown on Sauté mode for about 8 minutes then remove the bacon without the fat onto a plate using a slotted spoon. Set aside.
- Pour the mushroom into the pot, season it with salt and cook it for 5 minutes.
- Then, remove them onto the side of the bacon and set aside.

- Remove the chicken from the refrigerator onto a clean flat surface.
- Take out and discard the thyme but reserve the marinade.
- Pat the chicken dry with paper towels.
- Back to the pot, add half of the butter.
- Once it has melted, place the chicken in the butter in batches and fry them to become a dark golden brown color on each side. About 12 minutes.
- Add the bacon, mushrooms, shallots, garlic, carrots, and a bit of salt.
- Cook the ingredients for 4 minutes and top it with the wine and remaining thyme.
- Close the lid, secure the pressure valve, and select Poultry mode on High pressure for 15 minutes.
- Meanwhile, add the flour and the remaining butter in a bowl and smash them together with a fork. Set aside.
- Once the timer has ended, do a natural pressure release for 10 minutes, then a quick pressure release to let the remaining steam out, and open the pot.
- Plate the chicken and vegetables with a slotted spoon and set the cooker in Sauté mode.
- Discard the thyme.
- Add the flour mixture to the sauce in the pot, stir it until it is well incorporated.
- Cook for 4 minutes and adjust the seasoning with salt.
- Turn off the pot and spoon the sauce over the chicken.
- Garnish it with parsley and serve with steamed asparagus.

Nutrition facts per serving:

Calories 422; Fat 22g; Sodium 440mg; Carbs 15.2g; Protein 32g

Coconut Chicken Curry

You will love the color of this dish as it exudes excitement and healthiness. It cooks very fast, so this qualifies for a real hungry girl recipe. Make sure to use firm and fresh vegetables to give you the beautiful colors the dish should have as well as some crunch and fresh tastes.

Preparation Time: 12 minutes | Cooking Time: 20 minutes | Servings: 4

Ingredients:

4 Chicken Breasts
4 tbsp Red Curry Paste
½ cup Chicken Broth
2 cups Coconut Milk
4 tbsp Sugar
Salt and Black Pepper to taste
2 Red Bell Pepper, seeded and cut in 2-inch sliced
2 Yellow Bell Pepper, seeded and cut in 2-inch slices
2 cup Green Beans, cut in half
2 tbsp Lime Juice

Directions:

- Open the Mueller Pressure Cooker, and add chicken, red curry paste, salt, pepper, coconut milk, broth and swerve sugar.
- Close the lid, secure the pressure valve, and turn the pot on. Select Poultry mode on High pressure for 15 minutes.
- Once the timer has ended, do a quick pressure release, and open the lid.
- Remove the chicken onto a cutting board and select Sauté mode.
- Add the bell peppers, green beans, and lime juice. Stir the sauce with a spoon and let it simmer for 4 minutes.
- Slice the chicken with a knife and add it back to the pot. Stir and simmer for a minute. Dish the chicken with sauce and vegetable into a serving bowl and serve with coconut flatbread.

Nutrition facts per serving:

Calories 643; Fat 44g; Sodium 540mg; Carbs 30g; Protein 42g

Easy Chicken Thighs in Tomato Sauce

You can call it a world passer simply because it works with so many kinds of dishes across continents and can be made just anywhere easily. Making it in the Mueller pressure cooker is rewarding, so you get to save a lot of time for your work deadlines.

Preparation Time: 5 minutes | Cooking Time: 25 minutes | Servings: 4

Ingredients:

4 Chicken Thighs, skinless but with bone
4 tbsp Olive Oil
1 cup Crushed Tomatoes
1 large Red Bell Pepper, seeded and diced
1 large Green Bell Pepper, seeded and diced
1 Red Onion, diced
Salt and Black Pepper to taste
1 tbsp chopped Basil
½ cup Chicken Broth
1 bay Leaf
½ tsp dried Oregano

Directions:

- Place the chicken on a clean flat surface and season them with salt and pepper. Turn on the Mueller Pressure Cooker, and select Sauté mode.
- Pour the oil in, once heated add the chicken. Cook them to brown on both sides for 6 minutes. Then, add the onions and peppers. Cook to soften them for 5 minutes.
- Add the tomatoes, bay leaf, salt, broth, pepper, and oregano. Stir using a spoon. Close the lid, secure the pressure valve, and select Poultry mode on High pressure for 20 minutes.
- Once the timer has ended, do a natural pressure release for 5 minutes, then a quick pressure release to let the remaining steam out. Discard the bay leaf.
- Dish the chicken with the sauce into a serving bowl and garnish it with the chopped basil. Serve over a bed of steamed squash spaghetti.

Nutrition facts per serving:

Calories 437; Fat 37g; Sodium 273mg; Carbs 8g; Protein 24g

Buffalo Chicken Soup

This soup is creamy, full of sharp flavor, and very VERY satisfying.

Preparation Time: 7 minutes | Cooking Time: 30 minutes | Servings: 4

Ingredients:

4 Chicken Breasts, boneless and skinless
½ cup Hot Sauce
2 large White Onion, finely chopped
2 cups finely chopped Celery
1 tbsp Olive Oil
1 tsp dried Thyme
3 cups Chicken Broth
1 tsp Garlic Powder
½ cup crumbled Blue Cheese + extra for serving
4 oz Cream Cheese, cubed in small pieces
Salt and Pepper, to taste

Directions:

- Put the chicken on a clean flat surface and season them with pepper and salt. Set aside. Turn on the Mueller Pressure Cooker and select Sauté mode.
- Pour in olive oil, once heated add the onion and celery. Sauté with constant stirring using a spoon until they are softened which is for about 5 minutes.
- Then, add the garlic powder and thyme. Stir and cook them for about a minute, and add the chicken, hot sauce, and chicken broth. Season them with salt and pepper. Close the lid, secure the pressure valve, and select Poultry mode on High pressure for 20 minutes.
- Meanwhile, put the blue cheese and cream cheese in a bowl, and use a fork to smash them together. Set the resulting mixture aside.
- Once the timer has ended, do a natural pressure release for 5 minutes. Take out the chicken on to a flat surface with a slotted spoon and use two forks to shred the chicken and return it to the pot. Select Sauté mode.
- Add the cheese to the pot and stir until is slightly incorporated into the sauce.
- Turn off the Mueller cooker and dish the buffalo chicken soup into bowls.
- Sprinkle the remaining cheese over the soup and serve with sliced baguette.

Nutrition facts per serving:

Calories 487; Fat 34.3g; Sodium 373mg; Carbs 8g; Protein 41g

Classic Tuscan Chicken

I can't get enough of Tuscan chicken on a lazy Saturday afternoon. It is filling while light for the body to help me drag my feet around in style. I like to add some more pepper flakes to it when I'm in the mood to feel high. Above all, this dish gets thumbs up always whenever it is enjoyed.

Preparation Time: 10 minutes | Cooking Time: 20 minutes | Servings: 4

Ingredients:

4 Chicken Thighs, cut into 1-inch pieces
1 tbsp Olive Oil
1 ½ cups Chicken Broth
Salt to taste
1 cup chopped Sun-Dried Tomatoes with Herbs
2 tbsp Italian Seasoning
2 cups Baby Spinach
¼ tsp Red Pepper Flakes
6 oz softened Cream Cheese, cut into small cubes
1 cup shredded Pecorino Cheese

Directions:

- Pour the chicken broth into the pressure cooker, and add the Italian seasoning, chicken, tomatoes, salt, and red pepper flakes. Stir them with a spoon.
- Close the lid, secure the pressure valve, and select Poultry mode on High pressure for 15 minutes.
- Once the timer has ended, do a quick pressure release, and open the lid.
- Add and stir in the spinach, parmesan cheese, and cream cheese until the cheese melts and is fully incorporated. Let it stay in the warm for 5 minutes.
- Dish the chicken over a bed of zoodles or a side of steamed asparagus, and serve.

Nutrition facts per serving:

Calories 576; Fat 44g; Sodium 245mg; Carbs 12g; Protein 45g

Gorgeous Chicken Fajitas with Guacamole

These chicken fajitas are made to be rich in flavor, so you enjoy the aroma that exudes from every ingredient. It is essential to use corn tacos else you'll be breaking the deliciousness rule. Make as much as you can and share. It is effortless to do.

Preparation Time: 10 minutes | Cooking Time: 20 minutes | Servings: 4

Ingredients:

2 lb Chicken Breasts, skinless and cut in 1-inch slices
½ cup Chicken Broth
1 Yellow Onion, sliced
1 Green Bell Pepper, seeded and sliced
1 Yellow Bell Pepper, seeded and sliced
1 Red Bell Pepper, seeded and sliced
2 tbsp Cumin Powder
2 tbsp Chili Powder
Salt to taste
Half a Lime
Fresh cilantro, to garnish

Assembling:

Tacos, Guacamole, Sour Cream, Salsa, Cheese, Cooking Spray

Directions:

- Open the Mueller Pressure Cooker, grease the pot with cooking spray and line the bottom with the peppers and onion.
- Lay the chicken on the bed of peppers and sprinkle them with salt, chili powder, and cumin powder. Squeeze some lime juice and pour the chicken broth on top of it. Close the lid, secure the pressure valve, and select Poultry mode on High pressure for 20 minutes.
- Once the timer has ended, do a quick pressure release, and open the lid. Dish the chicken with the vegetables and juice onto a large serving platter.
- Add the sour cream, cheese, guacamole, salsa, and tacos in one layer on the side of the chicken.

Nutrition facts per serving:

Calories 423; Fat 22.1g; Sodium 479mg; Carbs 9g; Protein 39.7g

Mediterranean Meatballs Primavera

Sometimes, meatballs are just what you need to boost your mood up. Make this easy meatball dish that goes with many types of sauces and vegetable sides. You can make some extra pieces and refrigerate them for a weekly meal pack.

Preparation Time: 10 minutes | Cooking Time: 20 minutes | Servings: 4

Ingredients:

1 lb Ground Chicken	1 ½ tsp Italian Seasoning
1 Egg, cracked into a bowl	1 Red Bell Pepper, seeded and sliced
6 tsp Flour	2 cups chopped Green Beans
Salt and Black Pepper to taste	½ lb chopped Asparagus
2 tbsp chopped Basil + Extra to garnish	1 cup chopped Tomatoes
1 tbsp Olive Oil + ½ tbsp Olive Oil	1 cup Chicken Broth

Directions:

- In a mixing bowl, add the chicken, egg, flour, salt, pepper, 2 tablespoons of basil, 1 tablespoon of olive oil, and Italian seasoning. Use your hands to mix them well and make 16 large balls out of the mixture. Set the meatballs aside. Turn on the Mueller Pressure Cooker, and select Sauté mode.
- Pour half teaspoon of olive oil into the pot, once it has heated add the peppers, green beans, and asparagus. Cook for 3 minutes while stirring frequently.
- After 3 minutes, use a spoon the veggies onto a plate and set aside.
- Pour the remaining oil in the pot to heat and then fry the meatballs in it in batches. Fry them for 2 minutes on each side to brown them lightly.
- After, put all the meatballs back into the pot as well as the vegetables. Also, pour the chicken broth over it.
- Close the lid, secure the pressure valve, and select Poultry mode on High pressure for 15 minutes.
- Once the timer has ended, do a quick pressure release. Dish the meatballs with sauce into a serving bowl and garnish it with basil. Serve with over cooked tagliatelle pasta.

Nutrition facts per serving:

Calories 378; Fat 19.2g; Sodium 340mg; Carbs 13g; Protein 26g

Greek-Style Stuffed Chicken

Spinach feta stuffed chicken is something you can have on a special dinner when you are unsure of what to make. The spinach brings a worth of nutrients to the table while the feta cheese balances the taste of blandness from the spinach.

Preparation Time: 10 minutes | Cooking Time: 20 minutes | Servings: 4

Ingredients:

4 Chicken Breasts, skinless
Salt and Black Pepper to taste
1 cup Baby Spinach, frozen
½ cup crumbled Feta Cheese
½ tsp dried Oregano

½ tsp Garlic Powder
2 tbsp Olive Oil
2 tsp dried Parsley
1 cup Water

Directions:

- Cover the chicken in plastic wrap and put them on a cutting board. Use a rolling pin to pound them flat to a quarter inch thickness. Remove the plastic wrap.
- In a bowl, mix the spinach, salt, and feta cheese and scoop the mixture onto the chicken breasts. Wrap the chicken to secure the spinach filling in it. Use some toothpicks to secure the wrap firmly from opening. Carefully season the chicken pieces with the oregano, parsley, garlic powder, and pepper.
- Turn on the Mueller Cooker, open the lid, and select Sauté mode. Add the oil, once heated add the chicken to it and sear them to golden brown on each side. Work in 2 batches. Remove the chicken onto a plate and set aside.
- Pour the water into the pot and use a spoon to scrape the bottom of the pot to let loose any chicken pieces or seasoning that is stuck to the bottom of the pot. Fit the steamer rack into the pot with care as the pot will still be hot.
- Transfer the chicken onto the steamer rack.
- Seal the lid and select Poultry mode on High pressure for 15 minutes.
- Once the timer has ended, do a quick pressure release. Plate the chicken and serve with a side of sautéed asparagus, and some slices of tomatoes.

Nutrition facts per serving:

Calories 417; Fat 27g; Sodium 410mg; Carbs 3g; Protein 33g

Sticky Barbecue Drumettes

It is football season every time, and some barbecued chicken will do you some good. Instead of starting a charcoal grill for some grilled chicken, how about this quicker way of making them using the Mueller pressure cooker. They get ready in 24 minutes.

Preparation Time: 5 minutes | Cooking Time: 24 minutes | Servings: 4

Ingredients:

2 lb Chicken Drumettes, bone in and skin in
½ cup Chicken Broth
½ tsp Dry Mustard
½ tsp Sweet Paprika
½ tbsp. Cumin Powder
½ tsp Onion Powder
¼ tsp Cayenne Powder
Salt and Pepper, to taste
1 stick Butter, sliced in 5 to 7 pieces
BBQ Sauce to taste
Cooking Spray

Directions:

- Pour the chicken broth into the Mueller Pressure Cooker and insert the trivet. In the zipper bag, pour in dry mustard, cumin powder, onion powder, cayenne powder, salt, and pepper.
- Add the chicken, then zip, close the bag and shake it to coat the chicken well with the spices. You can toss the chicken in the spices in batches too.
- After, remove the chicken from the bag and place them on the steamer rack and place the butter slices on the drumsticks.
- Close the lid, secure the pressure valve, and select Poultry mode on High pressure for 20 minutes.
- Meanwhile, preheat an oven to 350 F.
- Once the timer has ended, do a quick pressure release, and open the lid.
- Remove the chicken onto a clean flat surface like a cutting board and brush them with the barbecue sauce using the brush.
- Grease a baking tray with cooking spray and arrange the chicken pieces on it. Tuck the tray into the oven and broil the chicken for 4 minutes while paying close attention to them to prevent burning. Serve warm.

Nutrition facts per serving:

Calories 374; Fat 11.32g; Sodium 262mg; Carbs 2.85g; Protein 38.34g

Balsamic Thyme Chicken Thighs

Such a quick but taste-enhancing way to cook a chicken. This chicken dish is that kind you look forward to having after a hard day of work. It is rewarding of your efforts, and the whole family will dine well to it.

Preparation Time: 10 minutes | Cooking Time: 40 minutes | Servings: 4

Ingredients:

2 lb Chicken Thighs, bone in and skin on
2 tbsp Olive Oil
Salt and Pepper, to taste
1 ½ cups diced Tomatoes
¾ cup Yellow Onion
2 tsp minced Garlic
½ cup Balsamic Vinegar
3 tsp chopped fresh Thyme
1 cup Chicken Broth
2 tbsp chopped Parsley

Directions:

- With paper towels, pat dry the chicken and season with salt and pepper. Turn on the Mueller Pressure cooker and select Sauté mode. Warm the olive and add the chicken with skin side down. Cook to golden brown on each side which is about 9 minutes. Remove onto a clean plate.

- Then, add the onions and tomatoes to the pot and sauté them for 3 minutes while stirring occasionally with a spoon. Top the onions with the garlic too and cook them for 30 seconds, then, add the chicken broth, some salt, thyme, and balsamic vinegar. Stir them using a spoon. Add the chicken back to the pot.

- Close the lid, secure the pressure valve, and select Poultry on High pressure for 20 minutes. Meanwhile, preheat oven to 350 F.

- Do a quick pressure release. Select Sauté. Remove the chicken to a baking tray and leave the sauce in the pot to thicken for about 10 minutes.

- Tuck the baking tray in the oven and let the chicken broil on each side to golden brown for about 5 minutes. Remove it and set aside to cool slightly.

- Adjust the salt and pepper seasoning in the sauce and when cooked to your desired thickness, turn off the Mueller Pressure Cooker.

- Place chicken in a serving bowl and spoon the sauce all over. Garnish with parsley and serve with thyme roasted tomatoes, carrots, and sweet potatoes.

Nutrition facts per serving:

Calories 412; Fat 16g; Sodium 321mg; Carbs 13g; Protein 39g

Holiday Stuffed Full Chicken

Big size dinner soon? Get this zingy full chicken ready for the table in less than an hour. It is flavor packed and of course, very healthy and light to have in the evening.

Preparation Time: 4 minutes | Cooking Time: 47 minutes | Servings: 6

Ingredients:

4 lb Whole Chicken
1 tbsp Herbes de Provence Seasoning
1 tbsp Olive Oil
Salt and Black Pepper to season
2 cloves Garlic, peeled
1 tsp Garlic Powder
1 Yellow Onion, peeled and quartered
1 Lemon, quartered
1 ¼ cups Chicken Broth

Directions:

- Put the chicken on a clean flat surface and pat it dry using paper towels. Sprinkle the top and cavity of the chicken with salt, black pepper, Herbes de Provence, and garlic powder.
- Stuff the onion, lemon quarters, and garlic cloves into the cavity of the chicken. Open the Mueller Pressure cooker, and fit the steamer rack in it. Pour the broth into the pot and put the chicken on the rack.
- Close the lid, secure the pressure valve, and select Meat on High pressure for 30 minutes. Meanwhile, get a baking pan ready.
- Once the timer goes off, do a natural pressure release for 12 minutes, then a quick pressure release to let the remaining steam out, and press Cancel.
- Open the pot and remove the chicken onto a prepared baking pan.
- Preheat oven to 350 F and place the baking pan with the chicken in it when it is ready.
- Broil the chicken for 5 minutes to ensure that it attains a golden brown color on each side.
- Dish the chicken on a bed of steamed mixed veggies for dinner. Right here, the choice is yours to whip up some good veggies together as your appetite instructs you.

Nutrition facts per serving:

Calories 376; Fat 14g; Sodium 1040mg; Carbs 3g; Protein 53g

PORK

Exciting Pork Chops with Mushroom Gravy

Meant to be a simple gravy but the mushrooms give it more worth. This passes for something you can make for your special someone who will be excited to enjoy this dish.

Preparation Time: 5 minutes | Cooking Time: 30 minutes | Servings: 4

Ingredients:

4 Pork Chops
1 tbsp Olive Oil
3 cloves Garlic, minced
Salt and Pepper, to taste
1 tsp Garlic Powder
1 (10 oz) can Mushroom Soup
8 oz Cremini Mushrooms, sliced
1 small Onion, chopped
1 cup Beef Broth
1 sprig Fresh Thyme
Chopped Parsley to garnish

Directions:

- Turn on the Mueller Pressure Cooker and select Sauté mode. Add the olive oil, mushrooms, garlic, and onion. Sauté them while stirring occasionally with a spoon until the onions are translucent for 3 minutes.
- Season the pork chops with salt, garlic powder, and pepper, and add it into the pot followed by the thyme and broth. Seal the lid and select Meat mode on High pressure for 15 minutes.
- Once the timer has ended, do a natural pressure release for about 10 minutes, then a quick pressure release to let the remaining steam out.
- Select Sauté and add the mushroom soup. Stir it until the mixture thickens. Dish the pork and gravy into a serving bowl and garnish with parsley. Serve with a side of creamy sweet potato mash.

Nutrition facts per serving:

Calories 423; Fat 18.5g; Sodium 560mg; Carbs 13g; Protein 35.5g

Honey-Mustard Pork Tenderloin

It is amazing how this tenderloin cooks in very little time than expected and this should be the case when cooking meat to not kill the nutrients in the food. It is a combination of sweetness from the monk fruit sugar and sharpness from the vinegar, but in all, it is SUPER tasty.

Preparation Time: 10 minutes | Cooking Time: 20 minutes | Servings: 4

Ingredients:

2 lb Pork Tenderloin	1 tsp Sage Powder
2 tbsp Olive Oil	1 tbsp Dijon Mustard
¼ cup Honey	¼ cup Balsamic Vinegar
½ cup Chicken Broth	1 tbsp Worcestershire Sauce
Salt and Black Pepper to taste	½ tbsp Cornstarch
1 clove Garlic, minced	4 tbsp Water

Directions:

- Put the pork on a clean flat surface and pat it dry using paper towels. After, season it with salt and pepper. Turn on the pressure cooker and select Sauté.
- Heat the oil and put the pork in and cook it on both sides to brown it which is about 4 minutes in total. Remove the pork onto a plate and set aside.
- Add the honey, chicken broth, balsamic vinegar, garlic, Worcestershire sauce, mustard, and sage. Stir the ingredients and return the pork to the pot.
- Close the lid, secure the pressure valve, and select Meat on High for 15 minutes. Once the timer has ended, do a quick pressure release.
- Remove the pork with tongs onto a plate and wrap it in aluminum foil.
- Next, mix the cornstarch with water and pour it into the pot. Select Sauté mode, stir the mixture and cook it to thicken. Then, turn the pot off after the desired thickness is achieved.
- Unwrap the pork and use a knife to slice it with 3 to 4-inch thickness. Arrange the slices on a serving platter and spoon the sauce all over it.
- Serve with a syrupy sautéed Brussels sprouts and red onion chunks.

Nutrition facts per serving:

Calories 432; Fat 12.1g; Sodium 440mg; Carbs 21.2g; Protein 43.3g

Pork Roast with Herb Gravy

Tweak up a regular gravy with some coffee and be in awe at the aroma. I like the entire introduction of Italian seasoning and ranch dressing to this meat dish. It offers a different, off the usual kind of satisfaction.

Preparation Time: 5 minutes | Cooking Time: 20 minutes | Servings: 4

Ingredients:

- 2 lb Pork Roast, cut into 2-inch slabs
- 1 tbsp Italian Seasoning
- 1 tbsp Ranch Dressing
- 1 tsp Red Wine Vinegar
- 2 cloves Garlic, minced
- Salt and Pepper, to taste
- 1 small Onion, chopped
- 1 tbsp Olive Oil
- 2 tsp Onion Powder
- ½ tsp Paprika
- 2 cups Beef Broth
- 2 tbsp Cornstarch
- 2 tbsp Water
- Chopped parsley to garnish

Directions:

- Season the pork roast with salt and pepper and place them aside.
- In a bowl, add the Italian seasoning, ranch dressing, red wine vinegar, garlic, onion powder, and paprika. Select Sauté mode, and open the pot.
- Add the oil to the pot, once heated add the onion and sauté it until it is translucent. Pour the gravy mixture and broth into the pot and add the pork roast.
- Close the lid, secure the pressure valve, and select Meat mode on High pressure for 15 minutes.
- Once the timer has ended, do a quick pressure release, and open the pot.
- Remove the pork roast with a slotted spoon onto a serving plate.
- Mix the cornstarch with the water in a small bowl and add it to the sauce, and select Sauté. Stir and cook the sauce for 4 minutes, until thickens.
- Once the gravy is ready, turn off the pot and spoon the sauce over the pork.
- Garnish with parsley and serve with a turnip mash.

Nutrition facts per serving:

Calories 483; Fat 15g; Sodium 590mg; Carbs 23g; Protein 49g

Ginger and Garlic Pork Tenderloin with Soy Sauce

Ginger is one spice to always have in the kitchen when cooking an asian-style dish. It has incredible colon cleansing benefits that really aid you when you are losing weight. Combined with soy sauce in this pork dish, you can only expect a health pack into your system with pleasant aromas.

Preparation Time: 3 minutes | Cooking Time: 20 minutes | Servings: 4

Ingredients:

2 lb Pork Tenderloin
½ cup Soy Sauce
¼ cup Sugar
½ cup Water + 2 tbsp Water
3 tbsp grated Ginger
2 cloves Garlic, minced
2 tbsp Sesame Oil
2 tsp Cornstarch
Chopped Scallions to garnish
Sesame Seeds to garnish

Directions:

- Open the Mueller Pressure Cooker and add the soy sauce, sugar, half cup of water, ginger, garlic, and sesame oil. Use a spoon to stir them. Then, add the pork.
- Close the lid, secure the pressure valve, and select Meat mode on High pressure for 15 minutes.
- Once the timer has ended, do a quick pressure release, and open the pot.
- Remove the pork onto a serving plate and set aside.
- In a bowl, mix the cornstarch with the remaining water until smooth and pour it into the pot.
- Select Sauté, stir the sauce frequently and cook it until it thickens.
- Once the sauce is ready, serve the pork with a side endive salad or any steamed green combination of your choice. Spoon the sauce all over it.

Nutrition facts per serving:

Calories 478; Fat 19g; Sodium 1617mg; Carbs 13g; Protein 51g

Quick Pork Roast Sandwich with Slaw

Got some pork roast in the fridge and trying to make something quick on a lazy day? This sandwich recipe is for you! Cook them into a pulled pork style, load your buns with it, and munch away with no shame.

Preparation Time: 5 minutes | Cooking Time: 15 minutes | Servings: 8

Ingredients:

2 lb Chuck Roast
¼ cup Sugar
1 tsp Spanish Paprika
1 tsp Garlic Powder
1 White Onion, sliced
2 cups Beef Broth
Salt to taste
2 tbsp Apple Cider Vinegar

Assembling:

4 Buns, halved
1 cup White Cheddar Cheese, grated
4 tbsp Mayonnaise
1 cup Red Cabbage, shredded
1 cup White Cabbage, shredded

Directions:

- Place the pork roast on a clean flat surface and sprinkle it with paprika, garlic powder, sugar, and salt. Use your hands to rub the seasoning on the meat.
- Open the Mueller Pressure Cooker, add the beef broth to it, onions, pork, and apple cider vinegar. Close the lid, secure the pressure valve, and select Meat mode on High pressure for 15 minutes.
- Once the timer has ended, do a quick pressure release. Turn off the pot. Remove the roasts to a cutting board. Then, use two forks to shred them.
- In the buns, spread the mayo, add the shredded pork, some cooked onions from the pot, and shredded red and white cabbage. Top with the cheese.

Nutrition facts per serving:

Calories 387; Fat 21g; Sodium 450mg; Carbs 21.3g; Protein 27g

Terrific Homemade BBQ Ribs

A must do with your Mueller pressure cooker. You don't need a grill to enjoy a barbecue anymore. Right here, is an amazing option to make and guess what, your guests will be all finger licking when they have it.

Preparation Time: 7 minutes | Cooking Time: 35 minutes | Servings: 2

Ingredients:

½ lb rack Baby Back Ribs
Salt and Pepper to season
¼ cup Beef Broth
½ cup Barbecue Sauce
3 tbsp Apple Cider Vinegar

Directions:

- Turn on the Mueller Pressure Cooker and select Sauté mode.
- Pour the oil into the pot and as it heats, season the ribs with salt and pepper.
- Brown the ribs in the oil for 1 to 2 minutes per side.
- Pour the barbecue sauce, broth and apple cider vinegar over the ribs and use tongs to turn it to be well coated.
- Close the lid and pressure valve and set the pot in Steam mode on High pressure for 25 minutes.
- Once the timer goes off, do a natural pressure release for 15 minutes, then a quick pressure release to let out the remaining steam, and open the lid.
- Remove the ribs onto a serving platter and set the pot in Sauté mode to simmer until the sauce thickens, about 6 minutes.
- Use a knife to slice the ribs and over the sauce all over it.
- Serve the ribs with a generous side of steamed but crunchy green beans.

Nutrition facts per serving:

Calories 387; Fat 17g; Sodium 670mg; Carbs 31g; Protein 24g

Heavenly Bangers with Mashed Potatoes & Onion Gravy

Bangers and mash are on my top list of convenient foods while offering the body with so many nutrients. Here's the tastiest recipe to find, make sure to make more for others too. It is that good!

Preparation Time: 5 minutes | Cooking Time: 35 minutes | Servings: 4

Ingredients:

2 lb Potatoes, peeled and halved
4 Italian Sausages
1 cup Water + 2 tbsp Water
⅓ cup Green Onion, sliced
Salt and Pepper, to taste
4 tbsp Milk

¼ cup + 2 tbsp + 2 tbsp Butter
1 tbsp Cornstarch
3 tbsp Balsamic Vinegar
1 Onion, sliced thinly
1 cup + 2 tbsp Beef Broth

Directions:

- Put the potatoes in the Mueller Pressure cooker and pour the water over it. Seal the lid; select Steam mode on High for 15 minutes. Do a quick pressure release, and open the lid. Remove the potatoes into a bowl.

- Add in a quarter cup butter and use a masher to mash them until the butter is well mixed. Slowly add the milk and mix it using a spoon. Add the green onions, season with pepper and salt and fold it in with the spoon. Set aside.

- Pour out the liquid in the pressure cooker and use paper towels to wipe inside the pot dry. Select Sauté mode and melt two tablespoons of butter. Brown the sausages on each side for 3 minutes. Remove to the potato mash and cover with aluminium foil to keep warm. Set aside

- Back into the pot add the two tablespoons of the beef broth to deglaze the bottom of the pot while stirring and scraping the bottom with a spoon. Add the remaining butter and onions; sauté the onions until translucent, then pour in the balsamic vinegar. Stir it for another minute.

- In a bowl, mix the cornstarch with water and pour it into the pot. Add the remaining beef broth. Allow the sauce to thicken and adjust the taste with salt and pepper. Turn off the heat once a slurry is formed. Dish the mashed potatoes and sausages in serving plates. Spoon the gravy over it and serve immediately with steamed green beans.

Nutrition facts per serving:

Calories 567; Fat 36g; Sodium 670mg; Carbs 45g; Protein 22g

Greek Tender Pork Roast

Yup! Something that doesn't take a struggle of the teeth to enjoy. This recipe takes a while with the good aim of tenderizing the pork so that it can be easily eating in a salad or a sandwich; or better still refrigerated and used in a stew. You will need about one hour for this but worth the time.

Preparation Time: 4 minutes | Cooking Time: 55 minutes | Servings: 6

Ingredients:

3 lb Pork Roast, cut into 3-inch pieces
3 tbsp Cavender's Greek Seasoning to taste
1 tsp Onion Powder
1 cup Beef Broth
½ cup Kalamata Olives, pitted
¼ cup fresh Lemon Juice
Salt (for extra taste, the Greek seasoning should be salty enough)

Directions:

- Open the Mueller Pressure cooker and put the pork chunks in it.
- In a bowl, add the greek seasoning, onion powder, beef broth, lemon juice, olives, and some more salt as desired. Mix using a spoon and pour the sauce over the pork.
- Close the lid, secure the pressure valve, and select Manual mode on High pressure for 45 minutes.
- Once the timer is done, do a natural pressure release for 10 minutes then do a quick pressure release to let out any more steam, and open the pot.
- Use a slotted spoon to remove the pork chunks onto a chopping board and use two forks to shred them.
- Add the shredded pork to a salad and serve.

Nutrition facts per serving:

Calories 478; Fat 22.41g; Sodium 288mg; Carbs 5g; Protein 52.95g

Braised Pork Neck Bones

I will recommend having this dish on the menu for a family get-together dinner. A little drizzle on steamed veggies is amazing. Then, with a broccoli mash, words can't explain the taste, and with rice, girl, you'll be up for a fantastic time.

Preparation Time: 4 minutes | Cooking Time: 35 minutes | Servings: 6

Ingredients:

3 lb Pork Neck Bones
4 tbsp Olive Oil
Salt and Black Pepper to taste
2 cloves Garlic, smashed
1 tbsp Tomato Paste
1 tsp dried Thyme
1 White Onion, sliced
½ cup Red Wine
1 cup Beef Broth

Directions:

- Turn on the Mueller Pressure Cooker, open the lid, and select Sauté mode.
- Pour in olive oil and while it heats, season the pork neck bones with salt and pepper. After, place them in the oil to brown on all sides. Work in batches for the best browning result. Each batch should take about 5 minutes.
- After, use a set of tongs to remove them onto a plate.
- Add the onion and sprinkle with some salt as desired. Stir with a spoon and cook the onions until they have softened. Then, add the smashed garlic, thyme, pepper, and tomato paste. Cook them for 2 minutes but with constant stirring to prevent the tomato paste from burning.
- Next, pour the red wine into the pot to deglaze the bottom of the pot. Add the pork neck bones back to the pot and pour the beef broth over it.
- Close the lid, secure the pressure valve, and select Meat mode on High pressure for 15 minutes.
- Once the timer has ended, let the pot sit for 10 minutes before doing a quick pressure release. Open the pot.
- Dish the pork neck into a serving bowl and serve with the red wine sauce spooned over and a right amount of broccoli mash.

Nutrition facts per serving:

Calories 487; Fat 36.5g; Sodium 329mg; Carbs 5g; Protein 33.4g

Gingery Pork with Coconut Sauce

The coconut and ginger in this dish bring out this exotic flavor, almost reminding you or making you dream of a beach? Vacation somewhere on the Indian Ocean. Well, don't dream too far, right there on your dining table, this dish creates that experience.

Preparation Time: 4 minutes | Cooking Time: 40 minutes | Servings: 6

Ingredients:

3 lb Shoulder Roast
1 tbsp Olive Oil
Salt and Black Pepper to season
2 cups Coconut Milk
1 tsp Coriander Powder
1 tsp Cumin Powder
3 tbsp grated Ginger
3 tsp minced Garlic
½ cup Beef Broth
1 Onion, peeled and quartered
Parsley Leaves (unchopped), to garnish

Directions:

- In a bowl, add the coriander, salt, pepper, and cumin. Use a spoon to mix them.
- Season the pork with the spice mixture. Then, use your hands to rub the spice on the meat.
- Turn on the Mueller cooker and open the pot. Add olive oil and pork to it.
- Add the onions, ginger, garlic, broth and coconut milk.
- Close the lid, secure the pressure valve, and select Manual on High for 40 minutes.
- Once the timer has stopped, do a quick pressure release, and open the lid.
- Dish the meat with the sauce into a serving bowl, garnish it with the parsley and serve with a side of bread.

Nutrition facts per serving:

Calories 491; Fat 31g; Sodium 237mg; Carbs 13g; Protein 38g

Mustardy Pork Loin with Vegetable Sauce

A bit of protein, a bit of good fat, and a bit of vitamins is what you have right here in this recipe. You can make some more steamed veggies to enjoy the sauce with or have it with a side of steamed green.

Preparation Time: 7 minutes | Cooking Time: 28 minutes | Servings: 4

Ingredients:

2 lb Pork Loin Roast
Salt and Pepper, to taste
3 cloves Garlic, minced
1 medium Onion, diced
2 tbsp Butter
3 stalks Celery, chopped
3 Carrots, chopped
1 cup Chicken Broth

2 tbsp Worcestershire Sauce
½ tbsp Sugar
1 tsp Yellow Mustard
2 tsp dried Basil
2 tsp dried Thyme
1 tbsp Cornstarch
¼ cup Water

Directions:

- Turn on the Mueller Pressure cooker and select Sauté mode. Pour in oil and while it heats quickly season the pork with salt and pepper.
- Put the pork to the oil and sear it to golden brown on both sides. Takes about 4 minutes. Then, include the garlic and onions and cook them until they are soft for 4 minutes too. Top it with the celery, carrots, chicken broth, Worcestershire sauce, mustard, thyme, basil, and sugar.
- Close the lid, secure the pressure valve, and select Meat mode on High pressure for 20 minutes. Once the timer has stopped, do a quick pressure release. Remove the meat to a serving platter.
- Next, add the cornstarch to the water, mix it smooth with a spoon, and add it to the pot.
- Select Sauté mode and cook the sauce to become a slurry with a bit of thickness. Adjust the taste with salt and pepper, and spoon the sauce over the meat in the serving platter. Serve with a side of steamed almond garlicky rapini mix.

Nutrition facts per serving:

Calories 543; Fat 26.1g; Sodium 360mg; Carbs 16g; Protein 55.7g

Pork Roast with Spicy Peanut Sauce

Peanuts are well-embraced ingredients in the American cuisine, and the combination with pork here brings a new kind of aroma that you will just love. Try it now and always!

Preparation Time: 8 minutes | Cooking Time: 20 minutes | Servings: 6

Ingredients:

3 lb Pork Roast
1 cup Hot Water
1 large Red Bell Pepper, seeded and sliced
Salt and Pepper to taste
1 large White Onion, sliced
½ cup Soy Sauce

1 tbsp Plain Vinegar
½ cup Peanut Butter
1 tbsp Lime Juice
1 tbsp Garlic Powder
1 tsp Ginger Puree
2 Chilies, deseeded, chopped

To Garnish:

Chopped Peanuts
Chopped Green Onions

Lime Wedges

Directions:

- Pour the soy sauce, vinegar, peanut butter, lime juice, garlic powder, chilies, and ginger puree to a bowl. Use a whisk to mix them together and even. Add a few pinches of salt and pepper, and mix it.
- Open the Mueller Pressure cooker and put the pork in it. Pour the hot water and peanut butter mixture over it.
- Close the lid, secure the pressure valve, and select Meat mode on High pressure for 20 minutes.
- Once the timer has stopped, do a quick pressure release, and open the lid.
- Use a slotted spoon or a set of tongs to remove the meat onto a cutting board and use two forks to shred it.
- Return it to the sauce and select Sauté mode. Let it simmer for about 2 minutes, then turn the Mueller pressure cooker off.
- On a bed of cooked rice, spoon the meat with some sauce and garnish it with the chopped peanuts, green onions, and the lemon wedges.

Nutrition facts per serving:

Calories 591; Fat 26.6g; Sodium 330mg; Carbs 20g; Protein 57g

Spiced Pork Carnitas in Lettuce Cups

Can't have a high carb burger, lettuce leaves are here to save. Make this flavorful pulled pork recipe and assemble them with grated carrots in the lettuce leaves. It is that simple to enjoy.

Preparation Time: 9 minutes | Cooking Time: 20 minutes + overnight refrigerated | Servings: 6

Ingredients:

3 lb Pork Shoulder
2 tbsp + 2 tbsp Olive Oil
1 small head Butter Lettuce, leaves removed, washed and dried
2 Limes, cut in wedges
2 Carrots, grated
1 ½ cup Water
1 Onion, chopped

½ tsp Cayenne Pepper
½ tsp Coriander Powder
1 tsp Cumin Powder
1 tsp Garlic Powder
1 tsp White Pepper
2 tsp dried Oregano
1 tsp Red Pepper Flakes
Salt to taste

Directions:

- In a bowl, add onion, cayenne, coriander, garlic, cumin, white pepper, dried oregano, red pepper flakes, and salt.
- Mix them well with a spoon.
- Drizzle over the pork and rub to coat.
- Then, wrap the meat in plastic wrap and refrigerate it overnight.
- The next day, turn on the Mueller Pressure Cooker, open the pot, and select Sauté mode.
- Pour 2 tablespoons of olive oil in the pot and once it is heating, remove the pork from the fridge, remove the wraps and put it in the pot.
- Brown it on both sides for 6 minutes and then pour the water on it.
- Close the lid, secure the pressure valve, and select Meat mode on High pressure for 20 minutes.
- Once the timer has stopped, do a quick pressure release, and open the lid.
- Use a set of tongs to remove the pork onto a cutting board and use two forks to shred it.
- Empty the pot and use some paper towels to wipe it clean inside.
- Set the pot in Sauté mode and add the remaining olive oil.

- Once it has heated, add the shredded pork to it and fry it until it browns lightly for 5 minutes. Turn off the heat and begin assembling.
- Arrange double layers of lettuce leaves on a flat surface, make a bed of grated carrots in them, and spoon the pulled pork on them.
- Drizzle a sauce of choice over them and serve with lime wedges on the side.

Nutrition facts per serving:

Calories 612; Fat 38.6g; Sodium 521mg; Carbs 10g; Protein 58.27g

Savory Ham with Collard Greens

Really simple recipe, but filled with a lot of good nutrients. It cooks in no time, so you needn't worry when you get trapped in hunger. Put everything together in the pot, hit start, and get your plate ready.

Preparation Time: 4 minutes | Cooking Time: 5 minutes | Servings: 4

Ingredients:

20 oz Collard Greens, washed and cut
2 cubes of Chicken Bouillon
4 cups Water
½ cup diced Sweet Onion
2 ½ cups diced Ham

Directions:

- Open the Mueller Pressure cooker and put the ham at the bottom of the pot.
- Add the collard greens and onion. Then, add the chicken cubes to the water and dissolve it. Pour the mixture into the pot.
- Close the lid, secure the pressure valve.
- Select Steam mode on High pressure for 5 minutes
- Once the timer has ended, do a quick pressure release, and open the lid.
- Spoon the vegetables and the ham with sauce into a serving platter.
- Serve with a side of steak dish of your choice.

Nutrition facts per serving:

Calories 178; Fat 3.5g; Sodium 527mg; Carbs 10g; Protein 26.5g

Creamy Ranch Pork Chops

Just five ingredients giving you creamy goodness, what else can you wish for? Put all the ingredients in the Mueller pressure cooker, hit Start, and rush to get a quick shower. On return, the dish will be near done to fill up your hungry tummy.

Preparation Time: 2 minutes | Cooking Time: 20 minutes | Servings: 4

Ingredients:

4 Pork Loin Chops
1 (15 oz) can Mushroom Soup Cream
1 oz Ranch Dressing and Seasoning Mix
½ cup Chicken Broth
Chopped Parsley to garnish

Directions:

- Open the Mueller Pressure cooker and add the pork, mushroom soup cream, ranch dressing and seasoning mix, and chicken broth.
- Close the lid, secure the pressure valve, and select Meat on High pressure for 15 minutes.
- Once the timer has ended, do a natural pressure release for 10 minutes.
- Then, do a quick pressure release to let the remaining steam out.
- Serve the pork and sauce with well-seasoned sautéed cremini mushrooms.

Nutrition facts per serving:

Calories 463; Fat 18.9g; Sodium 381mg; Carbs 14g; Protein 39.1g

BEEF RECIPES

Juicy Beef & Broccoli

One of the very first things you should make if you're in your early days of using your new Mueller pressure cooker. Beef and broccoli are a long existing recipe but the taste and nutrients derived never disappoint. So, you definitely should make it now and even often.

Preparation Time: 5 minutes | Cooking Time: 30 minutes | Servings: 4

Ingredients:

- 2 lb Chuck Roast, boneless and cut into thin strips
- 4 cloves Garlic, minced
- 7 cups Broccoli Florets
- 1 tbsp Olive Oil
- 1 cup Beef Broth
- 1 tbsp Cornstarch
- ¾ cup Soy Sauce
- Salt to taste

Directions:

- Turn on the Mueller Pressure Cooker, open the lid, and select Sauté mode.
- Add the olive oil, once it has heated add the beef and minced garlic. Cook the meat until it has browned.
- Add the soy sauce, and beef broth. Use a spoon to stir the ingredients well.
- Close the lid, secure the pressure valve, and select Meat mode on High pressure for 15 minutes.
- Meanwhile, put the broccoli in a bowl and steam it in a microwave for 4 to 5 minutes. After, remove it and set aside.
- Once the timer has ended, do a quick pressure release.
- Use a soup spoon to fetch out a quarter of the liquid into a bowl, add the cornstarch, and mix it until it is well dissolved.
- Pour the starch mixture into the pot and select Sauté mode. Stir the sauce and allow it to thicken into a slurry.
- Add the broccoli into the pot and let it simmer for 4 minutes. Dish the beef broccoli sauce into a serving bowl and serve with a side of cooked pasta.

Nutrition facts per serving:

Calories 355; Fat 12.8g; Sodium 506mg; Carbs 9g; Protein 41.8g

Russian Beefy Unstuffed Cabbage Stew

Very ideal for lunch, this sauce is heavy. A bit over a bed of pumpkin mash goes a long way to nourish your body. Kids may be picky on this one because of the big chunks of cabbage so make the vegetables in smaller cuts when there are kids.

Preparation Time: 8 minutes | Cooking Time: 21 minutes | Servings: 4

Ingredients:

1 cup Rice
1 large head Cabbage, cut in chunks
1 lb Ground Beef
Salt and Black Pepper to taste
½ cup chopped Onion
4 cloves Garlic, minced
2 tbsp Butter
1 Bay Leaf

1 cup diced Tomatoes
1 ½ cup Beef Broth
¼ cup Plain Vinegar
2 tbsp Worcestershire Sauce
1 tbsp Paprika Powder
1 tbsp dried Oregano
Chopped parsley to garnish

Directions:

- Open the Mueller Pressure cooker and set it in Sauté mode.
- Once the pot is ready, put the butter in it to melt and add the beef. Brown it for about 6 minutes and top it with the onions, garlic, and bay leaf. Stir and cook it further for 2 minutes.
- Pour in the oregano, paprika, salt, pepper, rice, cabbage, vinegar, broth, and Worcestershire sauce. Stir them well and let them cook for 3 minutes.
- Add the tomatoes but don't stir.
- Close the lid, secure the pressure valve, and select Manual mode on High pressure for 5 minutes.
- Once the timer is done, let the pot sit closed for 5 minutes and then do a quick pressure. Open the lid.
- Stir the sauce, remove the bay leaf, and adjust the seasoning with salt.
- Dish the cabbage sauce in serving bowls and serve with bread rolls.

Nutrition facts per serving:

Calories 521; Fat 15.31g; Sodium 369mg; Carbs 44.97g; Protein 38.81g

Hoagie Beef Burgers with Provolone Cheese

A great option to have for lunch using hoagies to certify your safety. It takes quite a while to make, but each bite is smooth because the meat has been tenderized for easy bites. Have fun making it with your choice of cheese, I used Provolone Cheese here, but you can try with any other.

Preparation Time: 5 minutes | Cooking Time: 60 minutes | Servings: 4

Ingredients:

1 tbsp Olive Oil
1 (14 oz) can French Onion Soup
1 lb Chuck Beef Roast
1 Onion, sliced
2 tbsp Worcestershire Sauce
2 Cups Beef Broth
Salt and Black Pepper to taste
1 tsp Garlic Powder
3 Slices Provolone Cheese
3 Hoagies, halved
3 tsp Mayonnaise

Directions:

- Season the beef with garlic powder, salt, and pepper. Turn on the Mueller Pressure cooker and select Sauté mode. Heat the olive oil and add the beef; brown it on both sides for about 5 minutes. Remove the meat onto a plate.

- Into the pot, add the onions and cook it to soften. Then, pour the beef broth into the pot and use a spoon to stir it while scraping the bottom of the pot off every stuck bit.

- Add the onion soup, Worcestershire sauce, and beef to the pot.

- Close the lid, secure the pressure valve, and select Meat mode on High pressure for 30 minutes.

- Once the timer has stopped, do a natural pressure release for 20 minutes, and then a quick pressure release to let out any remaining steam.

- Remove the meat onto a cutting board with tongs and use two forks to shred it. Strain the juice of the pot through a sieve into a bowl to be used as "Au Jus" for serving.

- Assemble the burgers by slathering mayo on halved hoagies, spoon the shredded meat over and top each hoagie with cheese. Serve with the "Au Jus" as a dip.

Nutrition facts per serving:

Calories 435; Fat 23.2g; Sodium 410mg; Carbs 9.3g; Protein 36.3g

Tricolor Pepper Rolled Beef with Onion Gravy

I'm one for aromas, and this beef dish exudes so much of it. Make it for lunch, for dinner or a festive celebration, and you'll be all cheers for putting in the effort.

Preparation Time: 20 minutes | Cooking Time: 42 minutes | Servings: 6

Ingredients:

2 lb Round Steak Pieces, about 6 to 8 pieces
½ Green Bell Pepper, finely chopped
½ Red Bell Pepper, finely chopped
½ Yellow Bell Pepper, finely chopped
1 Yellow Onion, finely chopped

2 cloves Garlic, minced
Salt and Pepper, to taste
¼ cup All-purpose Flour
2 tbsp Olive Oil
½ cup Water

Directions:

- Wrap the steaks in plastic wrap, place it on a cutting board, and use a rolling pin to pound it flat of about 2-inch thickness.
- Remove the plastic wrap and season them with salt and pepper. Set aside.
- Put the chopped peppers, onion, and garlic in a bowl and mix them evenly with a spoon. Spoon the bell pepper mixture onto the flattened steaks and roll them to have the peppers in it.
- Use some toothpicks to secure the beef rolls and dredge the steaks in the all-purpose flour while shaking off any excess flour. Place them in a plate.
- Turn on the Mueller Pressure Cooker, and select Sauté mode. Heat oil, and add the beef rolls and brown them on both sides, about 6 minutes.
- Pour the water over the meat, close the lid, secure the pressure valve, and select Meat mode on High pressure for 25 minutes.
- Once the timer has stopped, do a natural pressure release for 10 minutes, Remove the meat onto a plate and spoon the sauce in the pot over it. Serve the stuffed meat rolls with a side of steamed veggies.

Nutrition facts per serving:

Calories 396; Fat 21.5g; Sodium 540mg; Carbs 7g; Protein 46g

Asian-Style Red Beef Curry

This sauce is in a class of its own flavors and slightly different from the normal you often have. It gets ready in 30 minutes so you can plan to make it ahead before the hunger pangs set in.

Preparation Time: 5 minutes | Cooking Time: 33 minutes | Servings: 4

Ingredients:

1 ½ lb Beef Brisket, cut in cubes
1 tbsp Olive Oil
2 cloves Garlic, minced
¼-inch Ginger, peeled and sliced
2 Bay Leaves
2 Star Anises
1 large Carrot, chopped
1 medium Onion, chopped

2 tbsp Red Curry Paste
1 cup Milk
1 Potato, peeled and chopped
1 tbsp Sugar
2 tsp Oyster Sauce
2 tsp Flour
3 tbsp Water

Directions:

- Turn on the Mueller Pressure Cooker, open the lid, and select Sauté mode.
- Heat olive oil, and add the garlic, ginger, and red curry paste.
- Stir-fry them for 1 minute. Add the onion and beef. Stir using a spoon and cook for 4 minutes.
- Add the carrots, bay leaves, potato, star anises, sugar, and water. Stir.
- Close the lid, secure the pressure valve, and select Meat on High for 25 minutes.
- Once the timer goes off, do a quick pressure release.
- In a bowl, add the flour and 4 tablespoons of milk. Mix them well with a spoon and pour it in the pot along with the oyster sauce and remaining milk. Stir it gently to not break the potato.
- Cover the pot, select Sauté mode to allow the sauce to thicken for about 3 minutes. After, turn off the pot.
- Spoon the sauce into soup bowls and serve with a side of rice.

Nutrition facts per serving:

Calories 434; Fat 25.6g; Sodium 545mg; Carbs 24g; Protein 27.6g

Delicious Pepper Beef Mix

Anyone up for easy stir fry? There isn't the need to work up a stove top cooker to make this one. The Mueller pressure cooker gets it all done with peppers that are super crunchy.

Preparation Time: 5 minutes | Cooking Time: 48 minutes | Servings: 4

Ingredients:

2 lb Beef Chuck Roast
1 tbsp Onion Powder
1 tbsp Garlic Powder
1 tbsp Italian Seasoning
Salt and Black Pepper to taste, cut in 4 pieces
1 cup Beef Broth
1 medium White Onion, sliced
1 Green Bell Pepper, seeded and sliced
1 Red Bell Pepper, seeded and sliced
1 tbsp Olive Oil

Directions:

- Rub the beef with pepper, salt, garlic powder, Italian seasoning, and onion powder. Turn on the Mueller Pressure cooker and select Sauté mode.
- Add the oil, once heated add the beef pieces to it and sear them on both sides to brown which is about 5 minutes. Use a pair of tongs to remove them onto a plate after. (You can do this in 2 batches).
- Pour the beef broth and fish sauce into the pot to deglaze the bottom while you use a spoon to scrape any stuck beef bit at the bottom.
- Add the meat back to the pot, close the lid, secure the pressure valve, and select Manual mode on High pressure for 40 minutes.
- Once the timer has stopped, do a quick pressure release, and open the pot. Remove the meat to a plate and pour out the liquid in the pot out into a bowl.
- Use paper towels to wipe the inner part of the pot clean. Use two forks to shred the beef. Set aside.
- Select Sauté mode on the Mueller Pressure Cooker, add the remaining oil, once heated, add the beef with onions and peppers. Sauté them for 3 minutes and adjust the taste with salt and pepper.

Turn off the pot and dish the stir-fried beef into serving plates. Serve as a side to rice with sauce dish.

Nutrition facts per serving:

Calories 487; Fat 21.7g; Sodium 370mg; Carbs 10g; Protein 54g

Bacon Wrapped Beef with Green Beans

I like the idea of having this dish for a fancy dinner night coupled with a side of turnip or parsnip mash, some added sautéed veggies, and yourself to devour it. Add this recipe to the list of your special diets, and you can thank me later for the satisfaction.

Preparation Time: 5 minutes | Cooking Time: 23 minutes | Servings: 3

Ingredients:

3 Rib Eye Steaks
6 strips Bacon
Salt to taste
1 tbsp Olive Oil
2 cups long slices Green Beans
¼ cup Water

Special Tool:
Toothpicks

Directions:

– Season the rib eye steaks with salt. Roll around each steak with two bacon slices and secure the bacon ends with toothpicks.

– Turn on the Mueller Pressure Cooker, open the lid, and select Sauté mode. Add the wrapped steaks and brown them on both sides for 8 minutes.

– Then, add the green beans and pour the water them. Close the lid, secure the pressure valve, and select Meat mode on High pressure for 15 minutes.

– Once the timer has ended, do a quick pressure release. Plate the wrapped beef with the green beans and serve with a side of potato mash.

Nutrition facts per serving:

Calories 945; Fat 72g; Sodium 200mg; Carbs 21g; Protein 78g

Traditionally-Made Beef Bourguignonne

Don't worry if you don't drink. Some types of alcohol contain 0 making them perfect to use for cooking. Right here this beef burgundy (bourguignonne) sauce proves it all.

Preparation Time: 10 minutes | Cooking Time: 33 minutes | Servings: 4

Ingredients:

2 lb Stewing Beef, cut in large chunks
Salt and Pepper, to taste
2 ½ tbsp Olive Oil
¼ tsp Red Wine Vinegar
¼ cup Pearl Onion
3 tsp Tomato Paste
½ lb Mushrooms, sliced
2 Carrots, peeled and chopped
1 Onion, sliced
2 cloves Garlic, crushed
1 cup Red Wine
2 cups Beef Broth
1 bunch Thyme
½ cup Cognac
2 tbsp All-purpose Flour

Directions:

- Turn on the Mueller Pressure Cooker, open the pot, and select Sauté mode.
- Season the beef with salt, pepper, and a light sprinkle of flour. Add the oil to the pot, once heated add the meat and brown it on all sides.
- Can be done in batches but after all the meat should be returned to the pot.
- Pour the cognac into the pot and stir the mixture with a spoon to deglaze the bottom of the pot. Add thyme, red wine, broth, paste, garlic, mushrooms, onion, and pearl onions. Stir with a spoon.
- Close the lid, secure the pressure valve, and select Meat on High for 25 minutes.
- Once the timer is done, do a natural pressure release for 10 minutes, then a quick pressure release to let out the remaining steam, and open the lid.

- Use the spoon to remove the thyme, adjust the taste with salt and pepper, and add the vinegar. Stir the sauce and serve hot, with a side of rice (optional).

Nutrition facts per serving:

Calories 487; Fat 15.7g; Sodium 224mg; Carbs 14.2g; Protein 46.3g

Minute Steak and Cheesy Stuffed Mushrooms

Stuffed mushrooms are perfect when you want something light and easy for lunch, dinner, or even for brunch. What's exciting, you can use some leftover meat for it, and the Mueller pressure cooker will turn it into something incredible.

Preparation Time: 5 minutes | Cooking Time: 5 minutes | Servings: 3

Ingredients:

6 large White Mushrooms, stems removed
2 cups cooked Leftover Beef, cut in very small cubes
2 tsp Garlic Salt
½ cup Vegetable Broth
2 oz Cream Cheese, softened
1 cup shredded Cheddar Cheese
1 tsp Olive Oil

Directions:

- In a bowl, add the chopped beef, garlic salt, cream cheese, and cheddar cheese. Use a spoon to mix them.
- Spoon the beef mixture into the mushrooms and place the stuffed mushrooms in it. Drizzle them with the olive oil, and add the broth.
- Close the lid, secure the pressure valve, and select Manual mode on High pressure for 5 minutes.
- Once the timer has done, do a quick pressure release and open the lid.
- Remove the stuffed mushrooms onto a plate.
- Serve hot with a side of steamed green veggies.

Nutrition facts per serving:

Calories 315; Fat 17.5g; Sodium 142mg; Carbs 4g; Protein 24.3g

Savory Classic Pot Roast

With an ultimate dish like this on the table, you needn't yell to get everyone around. It smells so good and tastes fantastic. Make a good choice of beef, trim off any excess fat with a knife, and head up to begin cooking.

Preparation Time: 4 minutes | Cooking Time: 30 minutes | Servings: 4

Ingredients:

2 lb Beef Chuck Roast
3 tbsp Olive Oil, divided into 2
Salt to taste
1 cup Beef Broth
1 packet Onion Soup Mix
1 cup chopped Broccoli
2 Red Bell Peppers, seeded and quartered
1 Yellow Onion, quartered

Directions:

- Season the chuck roast with salt and set aside.
- Turn on the Mueller Pressure Cooker, open the lid, and select Sauté mode.
- Add the olive oil, once heated add the chuck roast and sear for 5 minutes on each side. Then, add the beef broth to pot.
- In a zipper bag add the broccoli, onions, peppers, the remaining olive oil, and onion soup.
- Close the bag and shake the mixture to coat the vegetables well. Use tongs to remove the vegetables into the pot and stir with a spoon.
- Close the lid, secure the pressure valve, and select Meat mode on High pressure for 25 minutes.
- Once the timer has stopped, do a quick pressure release, and open the pot.
- Remove the beef onto a cutting board, let it cool slightly, and then slice it.
- Plate and serve with the vegetables and a drizzle of the sauce in the pot.

Nutrition facts per serving:

Calories 492; Fat 23.8g; Sodium 347mg; Carbs 9g; Protein 55.2g

Savory Beer Beef Stew

Another way to tweak things around if you are not up for wines. Find a beer and use it for this dish. Trust me, the aromas and tastes differ, and you will be glad that you tried it.

Preparation Time: 10 minutes | Cooking Time: 50 minutes | Servings: 4

Ingredients:

2 lb Beef Stew, cut into bite-size pieces
Salt and Black Pepper to taste
¼ cup All-purpose Flour
3 tbsp Butter
2 tbsp Worcestershire Sauce
2 cloves Garlic, minced
1 packet Dry Onion Soup Mix
2 cups Beef Broth
1 medium bottle Beer
1 tbsp Tomato Paste

Directions:

- In a zipper bag, add the beef, salt, all-purpose flour, and pepper. Close the bag up and shake it to coat the meat well with the mixture.
- Turn on the Mueller Pressure Cooker, open the lid and Select Sauté mode.
- Add the butter, once it has melted add the beef and brown them on both sides for 5 minutes. Add the meat to deglaze the bottom of the pot.
- Stir in tomato paste, beer, Worcestershire sauce, and the onion soup mix.
- Close the lid, secure the pressure valve, and select Manual mode on High pressure for 35 minutes.
- Once the timer is done, do a natural pressure release for 10 minutes, and then a quick pressure release to let out any remaining steam.
- Spoon the beef stew into serving bowls and serve with over a bed of vegetable mash with steamed greens.

Nutrition facts per serving:

Calories 428; Fat 18.2g; Sodium 408mg; Carbs 15.2g; Protein 48.5g

Beef Meatballs in Spaghetti Sauce

Having a Mueller pressure cooker without making a meatball sauce is not permissible. You need to make this once and many times for yourself and your guests. Make sure to prepare some squash spaghetti as a side dish for it. I have a recipe shared below to help you in making it.

Preparation Time: 5 minutes | Cooking Time: 11 minutes | Servings: 6

Ingredients:

2 lb Ground Beef
1 cup Breadcrumbs
1 Onion, finely chopped
2 cloves Garlic, minced
Salt and Pepper, to taste
1 tsp dried Oregano
3 tbsp Milk
1 cuo Water
1 cup grated Parmesan Cheese
2 Eggs, cracked into a bowl
4 cups Spaghetti Sauce
1 tbsp Olive Oil

Directions:

- In a bowl, put it in the beef, onion, breadcrumbs, parmesan cheese, eggs, garlic, milk, salt, oregano, and pepper.
- Use your hands to mix the mixture and make bite size balls out of the mix.
- Open the pot, add the spaghetti sauce, water and the meatballs.
- Close the lid, secure the pressure valve, and select Steam mode on High pressure for 6 minutes.
- Once the timer is done, do a natural pressure release for 5 minutes, then do a quick pressure release to let out any extra steam, and open the lid.
- Dish the meatball sauce over cooked pasta and serve.

Nutrition facts per serving:

Calories 494; Fat 17.3g; Sodium 329mg; Carbs 18.1g; Protein 47.3g

Original Beef Burger with Cheddar

Something very handy to be able to make always. Burgers are a quick way of cooling impromptu hunger pangs, and this recipe makes it tasty enough to make you enjoy every bite.

Preparation Time: 5 minutes | Cooking Time: 15 minutes | Servings: 4

Ingredients:

1 lb Ground Beef
1 (1 oz) packet Dry Onion Soup Mix
1 cup Water

Assembling:

4 Burger Buns
4 Tomato Slices
4 Cheddar Cheese Slices
4 small leaves Lettuce
Mayonnaise
Mustard
Ketchup

Directions:

- In a bowl, add beef and onion mix, and combine them well together with your hands. Make 4 patties with your hands and wrap them in each foil paper.
- Pour the water into the Mueller Pressure cooker and fit the steamer rack in it. Place the wrapped patties on the trivet, close the lid, and secure the pressure valve. Select Chili on High pressure for 10 minutes.
- Once the timer has stopped, do a natural pressure release for 5 minutes, then a quick pressure release to let out the remaining steam.
- Use a set of tongs to remove the wrapped beef onto a flat surface and carefully unwrap them. Assemble the burger:
- In each half of the buns, put a lettuce leaf, then a beef patty, a slice of cheese, and a slice of tomato. Top it with the other halves of buns.
- Serve with some ketchup, mayonnaise, and mustard.

Nutrition facts per serving:

Calories 598; Fat 32g; Sodium 370mg; Carbs 35g; Protein 38g

Coconut Beef Roast

To tweak things up from the previous recipe, spice up the beef up with coconut and peanut to for a more exotic aroma. This dish goes well with a side of steamed asparagus and you may have a hot sauce on the side to kick things up.

Preparation Time: 5 minutes | Cooking Time: 35 minutes | Servings: 4

Ingredients:

1 lb Beef Roast, cut into cubes
Salt and Black Pepper to taste
½ cup Coconut Milk, light
½ cup Peanut Satay Sauce
2 cups diced Carrots

Directions:

- Open the Mueller Pressure cooker and place the beef inside.
- In a bowl, add the coconut milk, salt, pepper, and satay sauce.
- Use a spoon to mix them well and pour them over the beef.
- Add the carrots too.
- Close the lid, secure the pressure valve, and select Meat mode on High pressure for 25 minutes.
- Once the timer has ended, do a natural pressure release, then a quick pressure release to let out any remaining steam, and open the pot.
- Use a spoon to dish the meat into a serving plate.
- Serve with a side of steamed greens.

Nutrition facts per serving:

Calories 483; Fat 27.8g; Sodium 454mg; Carbs 19g; Protein 36.8g

Italian Pepperoncini Beef

Simple, saucy, flavor-packed dish to drool over. Although it takes a bit of time to make, it is worth the effort. Try your hands on this sweet flavored dish and pass the love around.

Preparation Time: 5 minutes | Cooking Time: 50 minutes | Servings: 4

Ingredients:

2 lb Beef Roast, cut into cubes
14 oz jar Pepperoncini Peppers, with liquid
1 pack Brown Gravy Mix
½ cup Water
1 pack Italian Salad Dressing Mix

Directions:

- Open the Mueller Pressure Cooker and put in the beef, pepperoncini peppers, brown gravy mix, Italian salad dressing mix, and water.
- Close the lid, secure the pressure valve, and select Manual mode on High pressure for 55 minutes.
- The goal is to make the beef very tender.
- Once the timer has stopped, do a quick pressure release, and open the pot.
- Dish the ingredients in the pot into a bowl and use two forks to shred the beef.
- Serve beef sauce in plates with a side of steamed veggies, a veggie mash, or bread.

Nutrition facts per serving:

Calories 415; Fat 18g; Sodium 350mg; Carbs 5g; Protein 47g

FISH RECIPES

Spicy and Sweet Mahi Mahi

It is not surprising that a pretty colored fish like this tastes great in turn. Mahi Mahi works well with different spices, ginger, cumin, fruity flavors, sweet sauce, and peppers. Top with a drizzle of melted butter and the evening will be fulfilling.

Preparation Time: 5 minutes | Cooking Time: 5 minutes | Servings: 4

Ingredients:

4 Mahi Mahi Fillets, fresh
4 cloves Garlic, minced
1 ¼ -inch Ginger, grated
Salt and Black Pepper
2 tbsp Chili Powder
1 tbsp Sriracha Sauce
1 ½ tbsp Maple Syrup
1 Lime, juiced
1 cup Water

Directions:

- Place mahi mahi on a plate and season with salt and pepper on both sides.
- In a bowl, add the garlic, ginger, chili powder, sriracha sauce, maple syrup, and lime juice. Use a spoon to mix it.
- With a brush, apply the hot sauce mixture on the fillet.
- Then, open the Mueller Pressure Cooker, pour the water into it and fit the trivet at the bottom of the pot. Put the fillets on the trivet.
- Close the lid, secure the pressure valve, and select Steam mode on High pressure for 5 minutes.
- Once the timer has ended, do a quick pressure release, and open the lid. Use a set of tongs to remove the mahi mahi onto serving plates. Serve with steamed or braised asparagus.

Nutrition facts per serving:

Calories 291; Fat 12g; Sodium 280mg; Carbs 20g; Protein 24g

Pernod-Flavored Mackerel & Vegetables en Papillote

Mackerels are high in omega-3 fatty acids which contain all those good fats that all your body yells for. I love making fish packs because of their exotic feel and the freshness in taste that they come with.

Preparation Time: 20 minutes | Cooking Time: 5 minutes + 2 hours for marinating | Servings: 6

Ingredients:

3 large Whole Mackerel, cut into 2 pieces
1 pound Asparagus, trimmed
1 Carrot, cut into sticks
1 Celery stalk, cut into sticks
½ cup Butter, at room temperature
6 medium Tomatoes, quartered
1 large Brown Onion, sliced thinly
1 Orange Bell Pepper, seeded and cut into sticks
Salt and Black Pepper to taste
2 ½ tbsp Pernod
3 cloves Garlic, minced
2 Lemons, cut into wedges
1 ½ cups Water

Directions:

- Cut out 6 pieces of parchment paper a little longer and wider than a piece of fish with kitchen scissors. Then, cut out 6 pieces of foil slightly longer than the parchment papers. Lay the foil wraps on a flat surface and place each parchment paper on each aluminium foil.
- In a bowl, add the tomatoes, onions, garlic, bell pepper, pernod, butter, asparagus, carrot, celery, salt, and pepper. Use a spoon to mix them.
- Place each fish piece on the layer of parchment and foil wraps. Spoon the vegetable mixture on each fish. Then, wrap the fish and place the fish packets in the refrigerator to marinate for 2 hours. Remove the fish to a flat surface.
- Open the Mueller Pressure Cooker, pour the water into it and fit the trivet at the bottom of the pot. Put the packets on the trivet. Seal the lid and select Steam mode on High pressure for 5 minutes.
- Once the timer has ended, do a quick pressure release, and open the lid. Remove the trivet with the fish packets onto a flat surface.
- Carefully open the foil and using a spatula, transfer the fish with vegetables to serving plates. Serve with a side of the lemon wedges.

Nutrition facts per serving:

Calories 285; Fat 15.3g; Sodium 44mg; Carbs 15g; Protein 14.9g

One-Pot Monk Fish with Power Greens

Luxury in one pot is what this recipe is. It is rich in greens and very good nutrients. For someone like me who is crazy about seafood, I will easily make it my go-to any day and I think you will love it the same way, if not more.

Preparation Time: 7 minutes | Cooking Time: 15 minutes | Servings: 4

Ingredients:

2 tbsp Olive Oil
4 (8 oz) Monk Fish Fillets, cut in 2 pieces each
½ cup chopped Green Beans
2 cloves Garlic, sliced
1 cup Kale Leaves
½ lb Baby Bok Choy, stems removed and chopped largely
1 Lemon, zested and juiced
Lemon Wedges to serve
Salt and White Pepper to taste

Directions:

- Turn on the Mueller Pressure Cooker, open the lid, and select Sauté mode.
- Pour in the coconut oil, garlic, red chili, and green beans. Stir fry for 5 minutes.
- Add the kale leaves, and cook them to wilt which is about 3 minutes.
- Meanwhile, place the fish on a plate and season them with salt, white pepper, and lemon zest. After, remove the green beans and kale into a plate and set aside.
- Back to the pot, add the olive oil and fish to it. Cook them to brown on each side for about 2 minutes and then add the bok choy to it.
- Pour the lemon juice over the fish and gently stir. Cook for 2 minutes and then turn off the Mueller Pressure Cooker.
- Spoon the fish with bok choy over the green beans and kale.
- Serve with a side of lemon wedges and there, you have a complete meal.

Nutrition facts per serving:

Calories 277; Fat 17g; Sodium 295mg; Carbs 19.4g; Protein 12g

Lime-Saucy Salmon

Salmon is very good in taste and nutrients. So, in this zingy sauce made to cook in just 5 minutes, I bet you will make it often. Feel free to add a kick of spice to this dish if you will like something hot for the tongue.

Preparation Time: 5 minutes | Cooking Time: 5 minutes | Servings: 4

Ingredients:

4 (5 oz) Salmon Filets
1 cup Water
Salt and Black Pepper to taste
2 tsp Cumin Powder
1 ½ tsp Paprika
2 tbsp chopped Parsley
2 tbsp Olive Oil
2 tbsp Hot Water
1 tbsp Maple Syrup
2 cloves Garlic, minced
1 Lime, juiced

Directions:

- In a bowl, add the cumin, paprika, parsley, olive oil, hot water, maple syrup, garlic, and lime juice. Mix them together with a whisk. Set aside.
- Open the Mueller Pressure cooker and pour the water into it. Then, fit the steamer rack in it. Season the salmon with pepper and salt; place on the steamer rack in the pot.
- Close the lid, secure the pressure valve, and select Steam mode on High pressure for 5 minutes.
- Once the timer has ended, do a quick pressure release, and open the pot.
- Use a set of tongs to transfer the salmon to a serving plate and drizzle the lime sauce all over it.
- Serve with steamed swiss chard.

Nutrition facts per serving:

Calories 564; Fat 32g; Sodium 150mg; Carbs 7g; Protein 64g

Fennel Alaskan Cod with Pinto Beans

Also known as the Pacific Cod, is a very mild flavored fish and allows all other forms of spices flavor it up just as you will desire. It is one of the best fish on the market to make and passes for a simple dinner or for when you want to impress.

Preparation Time: 4 minutes | Cooking Time: 21 minutes | Servings: 4

Ingredients:

2 (18 oz) Alaskan Cod, cut into 4 pieces each
4 tbsp Olive Oil
2 cloves Garlic, minced
2 small Onions, chopped
½ cup Olive Brine
3 cups Chicken Broth
Salt and Black Pepper to taste
½ cup Tomato Puree
1 head Fennel, quartered
1 cup Pinto Beans, soaked, drained and rinsed
1 cup Green Olives, pitted and crushed
½ cup Basil Leaves
Lemon Slices to garnish

Directions:

- Turn on the Mueller Pressure Cooker, and select Sauté mode. Heat the olive oil and add the garlic and onion. Stir-fry until the onion softened.
- Pour the chicken broth in and tomato puree.
- Let it simmer for about 3 minutes. Add the fennel, olives, beans, salt, and pepper. Seal the lid and select Steam mode on High pressure for 20 minutes.
- Once the timer has stopped, do a quick pressure release, and open the lid. Transfer the beans to a plate with a slotted spoon. Adjust broth's taste with salt and pepper and add the cod pieces to the cooker.
- Close the lid again, secure the pressure valve, and select Steam mode on Low pressure for 3 minutes.
- Once the timer has ended, do a quick pressure release, and open the lid.
- Remove the cod into soup plates, top with the beans and basil leaves, and spoon the broth over them.
- Serve with a side of crusted bread.

Nutrition facts per serving:

Calories 294; Fat 14.3g; Sodium 240mg; Carbs 26g; Protein 14.82g

SEAFOOD RECIPES

Chili-Garlic Black Mussels

When you're done making this dish, you will be as surprised as me when I first saw it too. It is colorful, bursting with flavor, and SUPER tasty. Get on with the fun but don't make it for yourself only.

Preparation Time: 15 minutes | Cooking Time: 30 minutes | Servings: 4

Ingredients:

1 ½ lb Black Mussels, cleaned and de-bearded
3 tbsp Olive Oil
3 large Chilies, seeded and chopped
3 cloves Garlic, peeled and crushed
1 White Onion, chopped finely

10 Tomatoes, skin removed and chopped
4 tbsp Tomato Paste
1 cup Dry White Wine
3 cups Vegetable Broth
⅓ cup fresh Basil Leaves
1 cup fresh Parsley Leaves

Directions:

- Turn on the Mueller Pressure Cooker, open the lid, and select Sauté mode.
- Add the olive oil, once heated add the onion and cook it to soften. Then, add the chilies and garlic, and cook it for 2 minutes while stirring frequently.
- Add the tomatoes and tomato paste, stir and cook it for 2 minutes. Then, add the wine and vegetable broth. Let it simmer for 5 minutes.
- Now, add the mussels, close the lid, secure the pressure valve, and select Steam mode on High pressure for 5 minutes.
- Once the timer has ended, do a natural pressure release for 15 minutes, then a quick pressure release, and open the lid.
- Remove and discard any unopened mussels. Then, add half of the basil and parsley, and stir.
- Dish the mussels with sauce in serving bowls and garnish it with the remaining basil and parsley.
- Serve with a side of crusted bread.

Nutrition facts per serving:

Calories 421; Fat 18g; Sodium 630mg; Carbs 23g; Protein 30g

Stylish Scottish Seafood Curry

I think I got exhausted with having meat curries and though with seafood this time around, the turnout was dope and I know you will say the same. It also gets ready in just 33 minutes rather than 2 hours that it will usually take on the stove top.

Preparation Time: 10 minutes | Cooking Time: 33 minutes | Servings: 8

Ingredients:

Seafood:

½ lb Squid, trimmed and cut into 1-inch rings
½ lb Langoustine Tall Meat
½ lb Scallop Meat
½ lb Mussel Meat

Curry:

4 tbsp Olive Oil
2 cups Shellfish Stock
2 Curry Leaves
2 tbsp Shallot Puree
3 tbsp Yellow Curry Paste
2 tbsp Ginger Paste
2 tbsp Garlic Paste
1 ½ tbsp Chili Powder
1 ½ tbsp Chili Paste
2 tbsp Lemongrass Paste
½ tsp Turmeric Powder
2 tsp Shrimp Powder
1 tsp Shrimp Paste
1 ½ cups Coconut Milk
1 cup Milk
1 tbsp Grants Scotch Whiskey
2 tbsp Fish Curry Powder
Salt to taste

Vegetables:

¼ cup diced Tomatoes
¼ cup chopped Onion

¼ cup chopped Okra
¼ cup chopped Eggplants

Directions:

- Turn on the Mueller Pressure Cooker, open the lid, and select Sauté mode.
- Add the olive oil, shallot paste, yellow curry paste, ginger puree, garlic paste, lemongrass paste, chili paste, shrimp paste, and curry leaves.
- Stir fry them for 10 minutes until well combined and aromatic.
- Next, top it with the turmeric powder, fish curry powder, and shrimp powder. Stir fry them for 1 minute.
- Pour in the shellfish stock and let it boil for 10 minutes.
- Then, add the scallops, squid, chopped onion, okra, tomatoes, and aubergine. Stir lightly.
- Close the lid, secure the pressure valve, and select Steam mode on High pressure for 5 minutes.
- Once the timer has ended, do a quick pressure release, and open the lid.
- Add the milk, coconut milk, scotch whiskey, and salt. Stir carefully to not mash the aubergine.
- Select Sauté and add mussel meat and langoustine.
- Stir carefully again.
- Simmer the sauce for 3 minutes and turn off the Mueller Pressure Cooker.
- Dish the seafood with sauce and veggies into serving bowls.
- Serve with a side of broccoli mash.

Nutrition facts per serving:

Calories 566; Fat 38g; Sodium 935mg; Carbs 42g; Protein 49g

Famous Carolina Crab Soup

Adding crab to a traditional creamy soup changes the aroma for the better. I pair this soup up with a side of crusted bread and it has never disappointed. Make it during the summer and winter seasons and it will serve just right.

Preparation Time: 5 minutes | Cooking Time: 40 minutes | Servings: 4

Ingredients:

2 lb Crabmeat Lumps	¾ cup Heavy Cream
6 tbsp Butter	½ cup Half and Half Cream
6 tbsp All-purpose Flour	2 tsp Hot Sauce
Salt to taste	3 tsp Worcestershire Sauce
1 White Onion, chopped	3 tsp Old Bay Seasoning
3 tsp minced Garlic	¾ cup Muscadet
2 Celery Stalk, diced	Lemon Juice to serve
1 ½ cup Chicken Broth	Chopped Dill to serve

Directions:

- Turn on the Mueller Pressure Cooker, open the lid, and select Sauté mode.
- Put the butter in to melt and then add the all-purpose flour and mix it in a fast motion to make a rue.
- Add celery, onion, and garlic. Stir and cook until soft and crispy, for 3 minutes.
- While whisking, gradually adds the half and half cream, heavy cream, and broth. Let it simmer for 2 minutes. Then, add the Worcestershire sauce, old bay seasoning, Muscadet, and hot sauce. Stir and let it simmer for 15 minutes. Add the crabmeat and mix it into the sauce well.
- Leave the Mueller Pressure cooker in Sauté mode and let the soup simmer for an additional 15 minutes. Then turn off the pot.
- Dish the soup into serving bowls, garnish with dill and drizzle squirts of lemon juice over it.
- Serve with a side of garlic crusted bread.

Nutrition facts per serving:

Calories 478; Fat 24.5g; Sodium 547mg; Carbs 18g; Protein 35.4g

Creamy Garlicky Oyster Stew

What better way to eat oysters than in a coconut celery fusion. A nutrient-packed stew that you can have with croutons to be filling. Oysters taste good in this delicious sauce, and I will have it over and over again.

Preparation Time: 3 minutes | Cooking Time: 8 minutes | Servings: 4

Ingredients:

2 cups Heavy Cream
2 cups chopped Celery
2 cups Bone Broth
3 (10 oz) jars Shucked Oysters in Liqueur
3 Shallots, minced
3 tbsp Olive Oil
Salt and White Pepper to taste
3 cloves Garlic, minced
3 tbsp chopped Parsley

Directions:

- Turn on the Mueller Pressure Cooker, select Sauté mode.
- Add the oil, garlic, shallot, and celery. Stir fry them for 2 minutes and add the heavy cream, broth, and oysters. Stir once or twice.
- Close the lid, secure the pressure valve, and select Steam mode on High pressure for 6 minutes.
- Once the timer has stopped, do a quick pressure release, and open the lid.
- Season with salt and white pepper. Stir and dish the oyster stew into serving bowls. Garnish with parsley and top with some croutons.

Nutrition facts per serving:

Calories 343; Fat 21.2g; Sodium 101mg; Carbs 12g; Protein 17g

Seared Scallops with Butter-Caper Sauce

Hanging with your special someone soon? Make this simple seafood to prove your culinary skills. It is so fast in the making, but the pleasant turn out looks better than the time put it.

Preparation Time: 4 minutes | Cooking Time: 12 minutes | Servings: 6

Ingredients:

2 lb Sea Scallops, foot removed
10 tbsp Butter, unsalted
4 tbsp Capers, drained
4 tbsp Olive Oil
1 cup Dry White Wine
3 tsp lemon Zest

Directions:

– Turn on the Mueller Pressure Cooker, open the lid, and select Sauté mode.
– Put in the butter and melt it to caramel brown. Use a soup spook to fetch the butter out into a bowl.
– Next, add the oil to the pot, once heated add the scallops and sear them on both sides to golden brown which is about 5 minutes.
– Remove to a plate and set aside.
– Pour the white wine in the pot to deglaze the bottom while using a spoon to scrape the bottom of the pot of any scallop bits.
– Add the capers, butter, and lemon zest. Use a spoon to gently stir the mixture once. After 40 seconds, spoon the sauce with capers over the scallops.
– Serve with a side of braised asparagus.

Nutrition facts per serving:

Calories 435; Fat 25.8g; Sodium 78mg; Carbs 2g; Protein 32.9g

VEGETABLES & VEGETARIAN RECIPES

Creamy Broccoli Mash

Make this creamy mash as often as you can to go with the different sauces and meat dishes that are shared here.

Preparation Time: 4 minutes | Cooking Time: 2 minutes | Servings: 4

Ingredients:

3 heads Broccoli, chopped
6 oz Cream Cheese
2 cloves Garlic, crushed
2 tbsp Butter, unsalted
Salt and Black Pepper to taste
1 cup Water

Directions:

- Turn on the Mueller Pressure Cooker, open the lid, and select Sauté mode.
- Drop in the butter, once it melts add the garlic and cook it for 30 seconds while stirring frequently to prevent the garlic from burning.
- Then, add the broccoli, cream cheese, water, salt, and pepper.
- Close the lid, secure the pressure valve, and select Steam mode on High pressure for 3 minutes.
- Once the timer has ended, do a quick pressure release and use a stick blender to mash the ingredients until smooth to your desired consistency and well combined.
- Adjust the taste with salt and pepper, and serve as a side dish to a sauce of your choice.

Nutrition facts per serving:

Calories 166; Fat 13g; Sodium 274mg; Carbs 5.6g; Protein 6.7g

Sweet Spaghetti Squash with Spinach-Walnut Pesto

It serves as spaghetti for when you crave original spaghetti but yet offers all the right nutrition you need. In 6 minutes, this faux spaghetti should be all-ready! Just sprinkle with the amazing Spinach and Walnuts-made Pesto and you'll fall in love with the veggie spaghetti.

Preparation Time: 5 minutes | Cooking Time: 6 minutes | Servings: 4

Ingredients:

4 lb Spaghetti Squash
1 cup Water

For the Pesto
½ cup spinach, chopped
2 tbsp Walnuts
2 Garlic Cloves, minced
Zest and juice from 1/2 lemon
Salt and ground pepper, to taste
⅓ cup extra virgin olive oil

Directions:

- In a food processor put all the pesto ingredients and blend until everything is well incorporated. Season to taste and set aside.
- Put the squash on a flat surface and use a knife to slice it in half lengthwise. Use a spoon to scoop out all seeds and discard them.
- Next, open the Mueller Pressure Cooker, pour the water into it and fit the trivet at the bottom.
- Place the squash halves on the trivet, close the lid, secure the pressure valve, and select Steam on High pressure for 6 minutes.
- Once the timer has ended, do a quick pressure release, and open the lid.
- Remove the squash halves onto a cutting board and use a fork to separate the pulp strands into spaghetti-like pieces.
- Scoop the spaghetti squash into serving plates and drizzle over the spinach pesto.

Nutrition facts per serving:

Calories 275; Fat 9.1g; Sodium 330mg; Carbs 46.1g; Protein 5g

Greek-Style Eggplant Lasagna

This dish poses as a faux lasagna but is cheesy tasty to the core. In 10 minutes or less, it gets ready and is perfect to enjoy by itself, or you may add it as a side to a meat dish. I prefer it to a pork dish.

Preparation Time: 8 minutes | Cooking Time: 8 minutes | Servings: 4

Ingredients:

3 large Eggplants, sliced in uniform ¼ inches
4 ¼ cups Marinara Sauce
1 ½ cups shredded Mozzarella Cheese
Cooking Spray
Chopped Fresh Basil to garnish

Directions:

- Open the pot and grease it with cooking spray.
- After, arrange the eggplant slices in a single layer in the bottom of the pot and sprinkle some cheese all over it.
- Arrange another layer of eggplant slices on the cheese, sprinkle this layer with cheese also, and repeat the layering of eggplant and cheese until both ingredients are exhausted.
- Lightly spray the eggplant with cooking spray and pour the marinara sauce all over it.
- Close the lid and pressure valve, and select Chili mode on High pressure for 8 minutes.
- Once the timer has stopped, do a quick pressure release, and open the lid.
- With two napkins in hand, gently remove the inner pot.
- Then, place a plate to cover this pot and turn the eggplant over on the plate.
- Garnish the eggplant and cheese with basil and serve as a side dish.

Nutrition facts per serving:

Calories 288; Fat 5g; Sodium 407mg; Carbs 38g; Protein 19g

Flavorful Leafy Green Sauté

Fun fact here: simple kale, swiss chard, and spinach are given an aromatic kick. With this, your meaty plates just got a lot more pleasant. Make sure to cook them not to be too wilted so that you can enjoy some crunch with as you bite on.

Preparation Time: 2 minutes | Cooking Time: 7 minutes | Servings: 4

Ingredients:

2 lb Baby Spinach
1 lb Kale Leaves
½ lb Swiss Chard
1 tbsp dried Basil
Salt and Black Pepper to season
½ tbsp Butter
½ cup Water

Special Tool:
Trivet with slings

Directions:

- Turn on the Mueller Pressure Cooker, open it, add the water to it, and fit the trivet at the bottom of the pot.
- Put the spinach, swiss chard, and kale on the trivet.
- Close the lid, secure the pressure valve, and select Steam mode on Low pressure for 3 minutes.
- Once the timer has ended, do a quick pressure release and open the lid.
- Remove the trivet with the wilted greens onto a plate and discard the water in the pot.
- Select Sauté mode on the pot and add the butter.
- Once it melts, add the spinach and kale back to the pot, and the dried basil. Season with salt and pepper and stir it.
- Dish the sautéed greens into serving plates and serve as a side dish.

Nutrition facts per serving:

Calories 130; Fat 3.5g; Sodium 165mg; Carbs 15g; Protein 13g

Winter Celeriac Pumpkin Soup

Looking for something that is a faux meaty soup? This vegetable soup will work well for you if you are a vegetarian. As you can see from the ingredients, they contain a great macros balance of carbs, fats, and protein.

Preparation Time: 15 minutes | Cooking Time: 13 minutes | Servings: 4

Ingredients:

1 Celeriac, peeled and cubed
16 oz Pumpkin Puree
5 stalks Celery, chopped
1 White Onion, chopped
1 lb Green Beans, cut in 5 to 6 strips each
2 cups Vegetable Broth
3 cups Spinach Leaves
1 tbsp chopped Basil Leaves
¼ tsp dried Thyme
⅛ tsp rubbed Sage
Salt to taste

Directions:

- Open the Mueller Pressure cooker and pour in the celeriac, pumpkin puree, celery, onion, green beans, vegetable broth, basil leaves, thyme, sage, and a little salt.
- Close the lid, secure the pressure valve, and select Steam mode on High pressure for 3 minutes.
- Once the timer has ended, do a quick pressure release and open the lid.
- Add the spinach and stir it in using a spoon. Cover the pot and let the spinach sit in for 3 minutes or until it wilts.
- Use a soup spoon to fetch the soup into serving bowls.

Nutrition facts per serving:

Calories 98; Fat 1.5g; Sodium 583mg; Carbs 14.6g; Protein 6.1g

Jeweled Quinoa-Stuffed Red Peppers

The Mueller pressure cooker makes stuffed peppers quickly so why not try this first to give you a hand around the pot if you are new to it? You will enjoy these stuffed peppers!

Preparation Time: 15 minutes | Cooking Time: 25 minutes | Servings: 4

Ingredients:

4 Red Bell Peppers
2 large Tomatoes, chopped
1 small Onion, chopped
2 cloves Garlic, minced
1 tbsp Olive Oil
1 cup Quinoa, rinsed
2 cups Chicken Broth

1 small Zucchini, chopped
1 ½ cup Water
½ tsp Smoked Paprika
½ cup chopped Mushrooms
Salt and Black Pepper to taste
1 cup grated Gouda Cheese

Special Tool:

Steamer Rack

Directions:

- Turn on the pot and select Sauté mode. Once it is ready, add the olive oil to heat and then add the onion and garlic. Sauté them for 3 minutes to soften, stirring occasionally.

- Include the tomatoes, cook them for 3 minutes and then add the quinoa, zucchinis, and mushrooms. Season them with paprika, salt, and black pepper and stir with a spoon. Cook them for 5 to 7 minutes, then, turn the pot off.

- Use a knife to cut the bell peppers in halves (lengthwise) and remove their seeds and stems.

- Spoon the quinoa mixture into the bell peppers leaving about a quarter space at the top of the peppers for the cheese. Sprinkle them with the gouda cheese. Put the peppers in a greased baking dish and pour the broth over.

- Wipe the pot clean with some paper towels, and pour the water into it. After, fit the steamer rack at the bottom of the pot.

- Place the baking dish on top of the steamer rack, close the lid, secure the pressure valve, and select Steam mode on High pressure for 15 minutes.

- Once the timer has ended, do a quick pressure release and open the lid.

- Remove the stuffed peppers and plate them.
- Serve right away or as a side to a meat dish.

Nutrition facts per serving:

Calories 409; Fat 16.9g; Sodium 240mg; Carbs 42g; Protein 19.8g

Steamed Asparagus with Pomegranate and Pine Nuts

Steamed asparagus bring a worth of taste to the plate, and they go well with almost any stew or chili that you can think of. There are quite a number of these shared under the stew section, feel free to do yourself some good.

Preparation Time: 2 minutes | Cooking Time: 3 minutes | Servings: 4

Ingredients:

1 ½ lb Asparagus, ends trimmed
Salt and Pepper, to taste
1 cup Water
¼ cup Pomegranate seeds
½ cup chopped Pine Nuts
1 tbsp Olive Oil to garnish

Special Tool:
Steamer Rack

Directions:

- Open the Mueller Pressure Cooker, pour the water into it and fit the steamer rack at the bottom.
- Place the asparagus on the steamer rack, close the lid, secure the pressure valve, and select Steam on Low pressure for 3 minutes.
- Once the timer is done, do a quick pressure release and open the lid.
- Remove asparagus with tongs onto a plate and sprinkle with salt and pepper.
- Scatter over the pomegranate seeds and pine nuts, and drizzle olive oil.

Nutrition facts per serving:

Calories 182; Fat 15g; Sodium 296mg; Carbs 13g; Protein 7g

Spicy Zoodle and Bok Choy Soup

This green zoodle soup satisfies me in tastes, nutrients, and flavor and is even healthier than the usual noodle soup.

Preparation Time: 15 minutes | Cooking Time: 17 minutes | Servings: 6

Ingredients:

1 lb Baby Bok Choy, stems removed
6 oz Shitake Mushrooms, stems removed and sliced to a 2-inch thickness
3 Carrots, peeled and sliced diagonally
2 Zucchinis, spiralized
2 Sweet Onion, chopped
2-inch Ginger, chopped
2 cloves Garlic, peeled
2 tbsp Sesame Oil
2 tbsp Soy Sauce
2 tbsp Chili Paste
6 cups Water
Salt to taste
Chopped Green Onion to garnish
Sesame Seeds to garnish

Directions:

- In a food processor, add the chili paste, ginger, onion, and garlic; and process them until they are pureed.
- Turn on the Mueller Pressure Cooker, open the pot, and select Sauté mode.
- Pour in the sesame oil, once it has heated add the onion puree and cook it for 4 minutes while stirring constantly to prevent burning.
- Add the water, mushrooms, soy sauce, and carrots. Stir.
- Close the lid, secure the pressure valve, and select Steam mode on High pressure for 3 minutes.
- Once the timer has ended, do a quick pressure release and open the lid.
- Add the zucchini noodles and bok choy, and stir them to ensure that they are well submerged in the liquid.

- Adjust the taste with salt, cover the pot, and let the vegetables sit for 10 minutes.
- Use a soup spoon to dish the soup with veggies into soup bowls.
- Sprinkle with green onions and sesame seeds.
- Serve as a complete meal.

Nutrition facts per serving:

Calories 115; Fat 6.1g; Sodium 46mg; Carbs 15g; Protein 2.1g

Fall Portobello Mushroom Pilaf

Fall is time to enjoy some tasty mushroomy pilaf. I reckon it will satisfy hunger pangs at the right moments.

Preparation Time: 5 minutes | Cooking Time: 23 minutes | Servings: 4

Ingredients:

2 cups Brown Rice, rinsed
4 cups Vegetable Broth
3 teaspoons Olive oil
1 cup Portobello Mushrooms, thinly sliced
Salt to taste
2 sprigs Parsley, chopped to garnish

Directions:

- Heat the oil on Sauté mode and cook the mushrooms for 3 minutes until golden.
- Season with salt and add rice and broth.
- Close the lid, secure the pressure valve, and select Chili mode on High pressure for 20 minutes.
- Once the timer has ended, do a quick pressure release and open the lid.
- Plate the pilaf, fluff with a fork and top with parsley and serve.

Nutrition facts per serving:

Calories 417; Fat 6.9g; Sodium 198mg; Carbs 71.8g; Protein 12.1g

Korean-Style Tofu Noddle Soup

Tofu is an all-time vegetarian favorite, and I possibly couldn't leave out a delicious recipe of it. So cheers to a happy moment making this delicious tofu soup. Before you begin, know that this soup is very aromatic and you could be found guilty of having too much of it.

Preparation Time: 10 minutes | Cooking Time: 15 minutes | Servings: 4

Ingredients:

16 oz firm Tofu, water- packed
7 cloves Garlic, minced
2 tbsp Korean red pepper flakes (gochugaru)
1 tbsp Sugar
1 tbsp Olive Oil
2 tbsp Ginger Paste
¼ cup Soy Sauce
3 cup sliced Bok Choy
6 ounces dry Egg Noodles
4 cups Vegetable Broth
1 cup sliced Shitake Mushrooms
½ cup chopped Cilantro

Directions:

- Drain the liquid out of the tofu, pat the tofu dry with paper towels, and use a knife to cut them into 1-inch cubes.
- Turn the Mueller Pressure cooker on, open the pot, and select Sauté mode.
- Pour the oil to heat, add the garlic and ginger, and sauté them for 1 minute.
- Add the sugar, broth, and soy sauce. Stir the mixture and cook it for 30 seconds. Include the tofu and bok choy, close the lid, secure the pressure valve, and select Steam on High pressure for 10 minutes.
- Once the timer has ended, do a quick pressure release and open the lid. Add the zucchini noodles, give it a good stir using a spoon, and close the lid. Let the soup sit for 4 minutes. Add the cilantro and stir it in with the spoon.
- Use a soup spoon to fetch the soup into soup bowls and enjoy.

Nutrition facts per serving:

Calories 354; Fat 15g; Sodium 489mg; Carbs 41.7g; Protein 21.2g

Restaurant-Style Parmesan Stuffed Mushrooms

Who says you can't have stuffed mushrooms without meat. Right here, this has been proven! It gets ready in 12 minutes and the chewy texture that comes with it is what will make you have it for days.

Preparation Time: 15 minutes | Cooking Time: 12 minutes | Servings: 4

Ingredients:

10 large White Mushrooms, stems removed
¼ cup Roasted Red Bell Peppers, chopped
1 Red Bell Pepper, seeded and chopped
1 Green Onion, chopped
1 small Onion, chopped
¼ cup grated Parmesan Cheese
½ cup Water
1 tbsp Butter
½ tsp dried Oregano
Salt and Black Pepper to taste

Directions:

- Turn on the Mueller Pressure Cooker, open the pot, and select Sauté mode.
- Put in the butter to melt and add the roasted and fresh peppers, green onion, onion, parmesan cheese, oregano, salt, and pepper. Use a spoon to mix them and cook them for 2 minutes.
- Spoon the bell pepper mixture into the mushrooms and use a paper towel to wipe the pot and place the stuffed mushrooms in it, 5 at a time. Pour in water.
- Close the lid, secure the pressure valve, and select Steam mode on High pressure for 5 minutes.
- Once the timer has ended, do a quick pressure release and open the lid.
- Use a set of tongs to remove the stuffed mushrooms onto a plate and repeat the cooking process for the remaining mushrooms.
- Serve hot with a side of steamed green veggies and a sauce.

Nutrition facts per serving:

Calories 80; Fat 4g; Sodium 190mg; Carbs 8g; Protein 5g

Winter Minestrone Soup

Remember to make this sauce as a saver for the cold nights. You can add a shake of hot sauce to it but most importantly, serve it warm to have the best satisfaction.

Preparation Time: 15 minutes | Cooking Time: 5 minutes | Servings: 4

Ingredients:

1 (15.5 oz) can Cannellini Beans
1 Potato, peeled and diced
1 Carrot, peeled and chopped
1 cup chopped Butternut Squash
2 small Red Onions, cut in wedges
1 cup chopped Celery
1 tbsp chopped Fresh Rosemary
8 Sage Leaves, chopped finely
1 Bay Leaf
4 cups Vegetable Broth
Salt and Pepper, to taste
2 tsp Olive Oil
2 tbsp chopped Parsley

Directions:

- Add in beans, potato, carrot, squash, onion, celery, rosemary, sage leaves, bay leaf, vegetable broth, salt, pepper, and olive oil.
- Close the lid, secure the pressure valve, and select Steam mode on High pressure for 5 minutes.
- Once the timer has ended, do a quick pressure release and open the lid. Add the parsley and stir it in with a spoon.
- Use a soup spoon to fetch the soup into soup bowls. Serve with a side of low crusted bread.

Nutrition facts per serving:

Calories 198; Fat 4.45g; Sodium 583mg; Carbs 27g; Protein 4.12g

Creamy and Greeny Soup

You will be surprised at the turn out of this kale blend. I never thought kale could taste this good until this recipe came about. I like very creamy stuff, so I take hold of the opportunity to make it creamy good and I think you will like it if you do same.

Preparation Time: 8 minutes | Cooking Time: 6 minutes | Servings: 4

Ingredients:

½ lb Kale Leaves, chopped
½ lb Spinach Leaves, chopped
½ lb Swiss Chard Leaves, chopped
1 tbsp Olive Oil
1 Onion, chopped
4 cloves Garlic, minced
4 cups Vegetable Broth
1 ¼ cup Heavy Cream
Salt and Pepper, to taste
1 ½ tbsp. White Wine Vinegar
Chopped Peanuts to garnish

Directions:

- Turn on the Mueller Pressure Cooker, open the pot, and select Sauté mode.
- Add the olive oil, once it has heated add the onion and garlic and sauté them for 1 minute. Add greens and vegetable broth.
- Close the lid, secure the pressure valve, and select Steam mode on High pressure for 5 minutes.
- Once the timer has ended, do a quick pressure release.
- Add the white wine vinegar, salt, and pepper. Use a stick blender to puree the ingredients in the pot.
- Stir in the heavy cream.
- Spoon the soup into bowls, sprinkle with peanuts, and serve.

Nutrition facts per serving:

Calories 269; Fat 14.2g; Sodium 431mg; Carbs 14.3g; Protein 12.5g

SNACKS & APPETIZERS RECIPES

Finger-Licking Barbecue Chicken Wings

Football season, movie night, or lazy day, these barbecued wings will satisfy your cravings. They are spicy with that kick to run your adrenaline high so make sure to use a cheesy to help tame the spiciness.

Preparation Time: 5 minutes | Cooking Time: 25 minutes | Servings: 6

Ingredients:

3 lb Chicken Wingettes

3 tbsp Cajun Garlic Powder

Salt to taste

¼ cup Barbecue Sauce

½ cup Hot Sauce

¼ cup Butter, melted

½ cup Water

Directions:

- Pat the wingettes with a paper towel and put them in a bowl. Season them with the Cajun garlic powder and salt.
- Open the Mueller Pressure Cooker, pour the water into it, and fit the steamer rack in it. Arrange the wingettes on the steamer rack. Close the lid, secure the pressure valve, and select Manual mode for 5 minutes. Press On/Start.
- Once the timer has ended, do a natural pressure release for 10 minutes, and then a quick pressure release to let out any more steam. Open the lid.
- Remove the wings with tongs into a bowl and add the butter, half of the hot sauce and half of the barbecue sauce to it. Stir the chicken until it is well coated in the sauce.
- Arrange the chicken on a wire rack and put it in an oven to broil at 350 F for 10 minutes. Remove the chicken into a bowl and add the remaining barbecue and hot sauces to it. Stir and serve the chicken with a cheese dip of your choice.

Nutrition facts per serving:

Calories 361; Fat 13.7g; Sodium 178mg; Carbs 9g; Protein 35.7g

Traditional Pao de Queijo

Just a big snack that you want to have by you just in case some hunger pangs pop in unexpectedly. You can also make them as appetizers to warm your guests up for a heavier meal being prepared.

Preparation Time: 15 minutes | Cooking Time: 20 minutes | Servings: 4

Ingredients:

2 cups All-purpose flour
1 cup Milk
A pinch to taste
2 Eggs, cracked into a bowl
2 cups grated Parmesan Cheese
½ cup Olive Oil

Directions:

- Grease the steamer basket with cooking spray and set aside.
- Put a pot on medium heat on a stove top. Add the milk, oil, and salt, and boil.
- Add the flour and mix it vigorously with a spoon.
- Turn off the heat and let the mixture cool. Once it has cooled, use the hand mixer to mix the dough very well and then add the eggs and cheese while still mixing. The dough will be thick and sticky after.
- Use your hands to make 14 balls out of the mixture and put them in the steamer basket and cover the basket with foil.
- Open the Mueller Pressure Cooker, pour the water into it, and place the steamer basket in it and cover it.
- Close the lid, secure the pressure valve, and select Chili mode on High Pressure for 20 minutes.
- Once the timer has ended, do a quick pressure release, and open the pot.
- Put the balls in a baking tray and brown them in a broiler for 3 minutes.

Nutrition facts per serving:

Calories 625; Fat 34g; Sodium 304mg; Carbs 54g; Protein 26g

Buffalo Chicken Balls with Roquefort Sauce

Buffalo goes with everything either as an appetizer or a sauce for the main meal. In 20 minutes, this dish should be ready to bite into. Enjoy with gladness!

Preparation Time: 10 minutes | Cooking Time: 20 minutes | Servings: 4

Ingredients:

1 lb Ground Chicken
2 tbsp Buffalo wing sauce
1 Egg, beaten
Salt and Pepper, to taste
2 tbsp Minced Garlic
2 tbsp Olive Oil
5 tbsp Hot Sauce
2 tbsp chopped Green Onions + extra for garnish

For the sauce:

½ cup Roquefort Cheese, crumbled
¼ tbsp Heavy Cream
2 tbsp Mayonnaise
Juice from ½ Lemon
2 tbsp Olive Oil

Directions:

- Mix all salsa ingredients in a bowl until uniform and creamy, and refrigerate.
- Add the ground chicken, salt, garlic, two tablespoons of green onions, and almond meal. Mix it with your hands.
- Rub your hands with some oil and form bite-size balls out of the mixture.
- Turn on the Mueller Pressure cooker and select Sauté mode.
- Add the remaining oil, and fry the meatballs in the oil in batches to brown.
- Meanwhile, add the hot sauce and butter to a bowl and microwave them until the butter melts. Mix the sauce with a spoon.
- Return the meatballs to the cooker and add hot sauce mixture and half cup of water.
- Close the lid, secure the pressure valve, and select Chili mode on Low Pressure for 10 minutes.

- Once the timer has ended, do a quick pressure release. Dish the meatballs.
- Garnish with green onions, and serve with Roquefort sauce.

Nutrition facts per serving:

Calories 424; Fat 38g; Sodium 204mg; Carbs 7g; Protein 26g

Party Egg Brulee

Instead of waiting for dinner and then having a crème brulee as dessert, you can make this egg version to be snacked on during your working hours. It is really simple and you can even teach the little ones that are good enough with an appliance to make them for themselves.

Preparation Time: 2 minutes | Cooking Time: 10 minutes | Servings: 8

Ingredients:

8 large Eggs
1 tsp Sugar
Salt to taste
1 cup Water
Ice Bath

Special Tool:
Steamer Rack, Hand Torch

Directions:

- Open the Pressure Cooker, pour the water in, and fit the steamer rack in it.
- Put the eggs on the steamer rack, close the lid, secure the pressure valve, and select Manual on High Pressure for 5 minutes.
- Once the timer has ended, do a quick pressure release, and open the pot.
- Remove the eggs into the ice bath and peel the eggs. Put the peeled eggs in a plate and slice them in half with a knife.
- Sprinkle a bit of salt on them and then followed by the swerve sugar.
- Turn on the hand torch and carefully brown the sugar on the eggs but not to burn the eggs. Serve with a spicy dip.

Nutrition facts per serving:

Calories 77; Fat 5.3g; Sodium 139mg; Carbs 1g; Protein 7.3g

Easy Tomato-Basil Dip

One more dip for you to add to your collection of dips for all your tasty veggie bites. Basil is full AMAZING aromas, I never get tired of it and sometimes I wish I could use it for everything, however, in this dip it proves itself to be in the high ranks of aromatic herbs.

Preparation Time: 5 minutes | Cooking Time: 13 minutes | Servings: 6

Ingredients:

1 cup chopped Tomatoes
¼ cup chopped Basil
10 oz shredded Parmesan Cheese
10 oz Cream Cheese
½ cup Heavy Cream
1 cup Water

Directions:

- Open the Mueller Pressure cooker and pour in the tomatoes, basil, heavy cream, cream cheese, and water.
- Close the lid, secure the pressure valve, and select Steam for 3 minutes at High.
- Once the timer has ended, do a natural pressure release for 10 minutes, then a quick pressure release to let out any remaining steam.
- Stir the mixture with a spoon while mashing the tomatoes with the back of the spoon.
- Add the parmesan cheese and stir it in until it melts.
- Dish the dip into a bowl and serve with chips or veggie bites.

Nutrition facts per serving:

Calories 350; Fat 28g; Sodium 120mg; Carbs 10g; Protein 13g

Bacon Wrapped Cheese Bombs

Just 3 ingredients and you should have something creamy and tasty to munch on anytime. These bacon bombs are not fattening so you have as much as you want.

Preparation Time: 10 minutes | Cooking Time: 12 minutes | Servings: 8

Ingredients:

8 Bacon Slices, cut in half
16 oz Mozzarella Cheese, cut into 8 pieces
3 tbsp Butter, melted

Directions:

- Wrap each cheese string with a slice of bacon and secure the ends with toothpicks. Set aside.
- Turn on the Mueller Pressure Cooker, open the lid, and select Sauté mode.
- Add the butter to melt it and add then add the cheese wrapped bacon to it.
- Fry them to brown and then remove them with a slotted spoon onto a paper-lined plate. Serve with a tomato dip.

Nutrition facts per serving:

Calories 230; Fat 13.5g; Sodium 310mg; Carbs 2g; Protein 24g

Honey-Mustard Sausage Weenies

Party food, appetizer or mid-day snack, these weenies are delicious and will go round with many requests for more.

Preparation Time: 15 minutes | Cooking Time: 3 minutes | Servings: 4

Ingredients:

20 Hot Dogs, cut into 4 pieces
Salt and Black Pepper to taste
1 tsp Dijon Mustard
1 ½ tsp Soy Sauce

¼ cup Honey
¼ cup Red Wine Vinegar
½ cup Tomato Puree
¼ cup Water

Directions:

- Add the tomato puree, red wine vinegar, honey, soy sauce, Dijon mustard, salt, and black pepper in a medium bowl. Mix them with a spoon.
- Put the sausage weenies in the cooker, and pour the sweet sauce over it.
- Close the lid, secure the pressure valve, and select Steam mode on High for 3 minutes.
- Once the timer has ended, do a quick pressure release. Serve and enjoy.

Nutrition facts per serving:

Calories 180; Fat 15g; Sodium 170mg; Carbs 14g; Protein 10g

Prosciutto Wrapped Asparagus

The Asparagus can be steamed and served not only as a side dish, but they can also be fused up to be snacked on. I love this easy fusion that gets ready in no time. Got a big task to finish? Make these wrapped asparagus and munch on them as you work. Trust me, and you will not feel the heat of the workload.

Preparation Time: 5 minutes | Cooking Time: 4 minutes | Servings: 6

Ingredients:

1 lb Asparagus, stalks trimmed
10 oz Prosciutto, thinly sliced
1 cup Water

Directions:

- Wrap each asparagus with a slice of prosciutto from the top of the asparagus to the bottom of it.
- Open the Pressure Cooker, pour the water in, and fit the steamer basket in.
- Put in the wrapped asparagus and then close the lid, secure the pressure valve, and select Steam on High Pressure for 4 minutes.
- Once the timer has ended, do a quick pressure release, and open the pot.
- Remove the wrapped asparagus onto a plate and serve with cheese dip.

Nutrition facts per serving:

Calories 154; Fat 12.4g; Sodium 240mg; Carbs 3g; Protein 9.4g

Crunchy Bacon Cheeseburger Dip

Need something to make chips tastier, then you should make this dip. The sound of bacon in a blend of cheese is mouthwatering already, and I think I might get this whooped up in a short while. Support the ideas? Do it too!

Preparation Time: 5 minutes | Cooking Time: 5 minutes | Servings: 10

Ingredients:

½ cup chopped Tomatoes
10 oz shredded Monterey Jack Cheese
10 oz Cream Cheese
10 Bacon Slices, chopped roughly
1 cup Water

Directions:

- Turn on the Mueller Pressure Cooker, open the pot, and select Sauté mode. Add the bacon pieces and cook them to brown.
- Use a spoon to fetch out the grease and add the water, cream cheese, and tomatoes. Do Not Stir. Close the lid, secure the pressure valve, and select Manual mode on High pressure for 5 minutes.
- Once the timer has ended, do a quick pressure release, and open the lid.
- Stir in the cheddar cheese and mix to combine. Serve with a side of chips.

Nutrition facts per serving:

Calories 353; Fat 25.3g; Sodium 88mg; Carbs 20.5g; Protein 7.9g

Cheesy Chicken Dip

Use this dip for all your veggie bites and the creamy effect will linger down your throat for hours. It is very straight forwarded to make, that's one reason why I love it!

Preparation Time: 3 minutes | Cooking Time: 1 hour 15 minutes | Servings: 6

Ingredients:

1 lb Chicken Breast
½ cup Breadcrumbs
10 oz Cheddar Cheese
½ cup Sour Cream
10 oz Cream Cheese
½ cup Water

Directions:

- Open the Mueller pressure cooker and add the chicken, water, and cream cheese.
- Close the lid, secure the pressure valve, and select Chili mode on High Pressure for 10 minutes.
- Once the timer has ended, do a quick pressure release, and open the pot.
- Add the cheddar cheese and shred the chicken with two forks.
- Spoon the dip into a baking dish, sprinkle with breadcrumbs, and place in a broiler to brown the top for 3 minutes. Serve warm with veggie bites.

Nutrition facts per serving:

Calories 387; Fat 26g; Sodium 302mg; Carbs 10.2g; Protein 27g

DESSERTS RECIPES

Holiday Chocolate Cheesecake

This is a kiddie special, and I bet that they will be all over you when you make them. The good thing is that you can make this dessert often for the entire family because it is made of healthy, non-fattening ingredients.

Preparation Time: 15 minutes | Cooking Time: 25 minutes + 6 hours for cooling | Servings: 8

Ingredients:

2 cups Water

Crust:

1 cup Graham Crackers Crumbs

1 tbsp Sugar

3 tbsp Cocoa Powder

3 tbsp Butter, melted

Filling:

2 Eggs, room temperature and cracked into a bowl

2 Egg Yolks, room temperature and cracked into a bowl

20 oz Cream Cheese, room temperature

½ cup Granulated Sugar

½ cup Cocoa Powder

1 cup Heavy Cream

½ cup Sour Cream

2 tsp Vanilla Extract

8 oz Baking Chocolate, melted

Needed Tool:

8-inch Spring Form Pan

Parchment Paper

Kitchen Scissors

Electric Mixer

Trivet with side slings

Aluminum Foil

Directions:

Start off with the crust:

- Line an 8-inch springform pan with parchment paper and use kitchen scissors to trim the paper to fit the pan.
- In a mixing bowl, add the graham crackers crumbs, cocoa powder, and sugar. Use a spoon to mix them evenly then add the melted butter and mix again until well incorporated.
- Spoon the mixture into the springform pan and tap it to firm it using the spoon. Set aside. Move on to the make the filling:
- Using an electric mixer, beat the cream cheese and cocoa powder.
- While still mixing, add the eggs and egg yolks.
- Once combined and still mixing, add the sour cream, melted chocolate, heavy cream, and vanilla extract.
- Use a spatula to scrape the sides of the bowl as you mix.
- Once well combined, turn off the electric mixer, and spoon the filling mixture onto the crust in the springform pan.
- Use the spatula to smoothen it out.
- Open the Mueller Cooker, and fit the trivet at the bottom of it and pour in the water. Loosely cover the springform pan with foil and place it on the rack.
- Close the lid, secure the pressure valve, and select Cake mode on High pressure for 10 minutes.
- Once the timer has stopped, do a natural pressure release for 15 minutes, then a quick pressure release to let out the remaining steam.
- With napkins in both hands, hold the trivet's sling and lift it out with the spring form pan.
- Let the cake sit for an hour to cool and then refrigerate for 5 hours.
- After the refrigeration is done, open the spring form pan and slice the cake.

Nutrition facts per serving:

Calories 513; Fat 48g; Sodium 56mg; Carbs 21g; Protein 14g

Easy Crème Brulee

I love crème brulee so much that it is my first choice dessert to pick when at the restaurant. Being able to make it quickly with the Mueller pressure cooker is very exciting so cheers to many days of CRÈME BRULÉE.

Preparation Time: 5 minutes | Cooking Time: 23 minutes + 6 hours of cooling | Servings: 4

Ingredients:

3 cups Heavy Whipping Cream
6 tbsp Sugar
7 large Egg Yolks
2 tbsp Vanilla Extract
2 cups Water

Directions:

- In a mixing bowl, add the yolks, vanilla, whipping cream, and half of the swerve sugar. Use a whisk to mix them until they are well combined.
- Pour the mixture into the ramekins and cover them with aluminium foil.
- Open the Mueller Cooker, fit the trivet into the pot, and pour in the water.
- Place 3 ramekins on the trivet and place the remaining ramekins to sit on the edges of the ramekins below.
- Close the lid, secure the pressure valve, and select Chili mode on High pressure for 8 minutes.
- Once the timer has stopped, do a natural pressure release for 15 minutes, then a quick pressure release to let out the remaining pressure.
- With a napkin in hand, remove the ramekins onto a flat surface and then into a refrigerator to chill for at least 6 hours.
- After refrigeration, remove the ramekins and remove the aluminium foil.
- Equally, sprinkle the remaining sugar on it and use a hand torch to brown the top of the crème brulee. Serve the dessert.

Nutrition facts per serving:

Calories 487; Fat 42.1g; Sodium 38mg; Carbs 23.2g; Protein 5.1g

Hot Lava Cake

Got a big group to serve? This drool deserving cake will go around well while satisfying everyone. The amazing thing about it is that it needs just six (6) ingredients to get ready.

Preparation Time: 10 minutes | Cooking Time: 29 minutes | Servings: 8

Ingredients:

1 cup Butter
4 tbsp Milk
4 tsp Vanilla Extract
1 ½ cups Chocolate Chips
1 ½ cups Sugar
Powdered sugar to garnish
7 tbsp All-purpose Flour
5 Eggs
1 cup Water

Directions:

- Grease the cake pan with cooking spray and set aside. Open the Mueller Cooker, fit the trivet at the bottom of it, and pour in the water.
- In a medium heatproof bowl, add the butter and chocolate and melt them in the microwave for about 2 minutes. Remove it from the microwave.
- Add sugar and use a spatula to stir it well. Add the eggs, milk, and vanilla extract and stir again. Finally, add the flour and stir it until even and smooth.
- Pour the batter into the greased cake pan and use the spatula to level it.
- Place the pan on the trivet in the pot, close the lid, secure the pressure valve, and select Cake on High for 15 minutes.
- Once the timer has gone off, do a natural pressure release for 12 minutes, then a quick pressure release, and open the lid.
- Remove the trivet with the pan on it and place the pan on a flat surface. Put a plate over the pan and flip the cake over into the plate. Pour the powdered sugar in a fine sieve and sift it over the cake. Use a knife to cut the cake into 8 slices and serve immediately (while warm).

Nutrition facts per serving:

Calories 460; Fat 23g; Sodium 240mg; Carbs 28g; Protein 9.5g

Lemon-Ricotta Cheesecake with Strawberry

Pamper yourself with this zingy creamy nourishment. I love cheese a lot, so this cake is what I could splurge on morning, noon, and night. After so much of it, you are rest assured to be in a healthy state as it digests quickly with little to no fattening properties to worry about.

Preparation Time: 10 minutes | Cooking Time: 25 minutes | Servings: 6

Ingredients:

10 oz Cream Cheese
¼ cup Sugar
½ cup Ricotta Cheese
One Lemon, zested and juiced
2 Eggs, cracked into a bowl

1 tsp Lemon Extract
3 tbsp Sour Cream
1 ½ cups Water
10 Strawberries, halved to decorate

Directions:

- In the electric mixer, add the cream cheese, quarter cup of sugar, ricotta cheese, lemon zest, lemon juice, and lemon extract. Turn on the mixer and mix the ingredients until a smooth consistency is formed. Adjust the sweet taste to liking with more sugar.

- Reduce the speed of the mixer and add the eggs. Fold it in at low speed until it is fully incorporated. Make sure not to fold the eggs in high speed to prevent a cracked crust. Grease the spring form pan with cooking spray and use a spatula to spoon the mixture into the pan. Level the top with the spatula and cover it with foil.

- Open the Mueller Pressure Cooker, fit the trivet in it, and pour the water in it. Place the cake pan on the trivet. Close the lid, secure the pressure valve, and select Cake mode on High pressure for 15 minutes.

- Meanwhile, mix the sour cream and one tablespoon of sugar. Set aside.

- Once the timer has gone off, do a natural pressure release for 10 minutes, then a quick pressure release to let out any extra steam, and open the lid.

- Remove the trivet with pan, place the spring form pan on a flat surface, and open it. Use a spatula to spread the sour cream mixture on the warm cake. Refrigerate the cake for 8 hours. Top with strawberries; slice it into 6 pieces and serve while firm.

Nutrition facts per serving:

Calories 241; Fat 20g; Sodium 156mg; Carbs 8g; Protein 9g

Beautiful Vanilla Pudding with Berries

So, right here at the end of this book lays an amazing surprise…STRAWBERRIES and BLUEBERRIES!!

Preparation Time: 15 minutes | Cooking Time: 18 minutes + 6h for refrigeration | Servings: 4

Ingredients:

1 cup Heavy Cream
4 Egg Yolks
4 tbsp Water + 1 ½ cups Water
½ cup Milk

1 tsp Vanilla
½ cup Sugar
4 Raspberries
4 Blueberries

Directions:

— Open the Mueller Cooker, and fit the trivet at the bottom of the pot, and pour one and a half cup of water in it.

— In a small pan set over low heat on a stove top, add four tablespoons for water and the sugar. Stir it constantly until it dissolves. Turn off the heat.

— Add milk, heavy cream, and vanilla. Stir it with a whisk until evenly combined.

— Crack the eggs into a bowl and add a tablespoon of the cream mixture. Whisk it and then very slowly add the remaining cream mixture while whisking.

— Pour the mixture into the ramekins and place them on the trivet in the Mueller Pressure Cooker.

— Close the lid of the pot, secure the pressure valve, and select Cake mode on High Pressure for 4 minutes.

— Once the timer has gone off, do a quick pressure release, and open the lid.

— With a napkin in hand, carefully remove the ramekins onto a flat surface. Let them cool for about 15 minutes and then refrigerate them for 6 hours.

— After 6 hours, remove them from the refrigerator and garnish them with the raspberries and blueberries.

— Enjoy immediately or refrigerate further until dessert time is ready.

Nutrition facts per serving:

Calories 183; Fat 12.9g; Sodium 350mg; Carbs 12g; Protein 4g

Made in the USA
Middletown, DE
14 December 2018